ALFRED A. KNOPF

1915 · 100 YEARS · 2015

Also by Joe Bastianich

Restaurant Man

Grandi Vini: An Opinionated Tour of Italy's 89 Finest Wines

Vino Italiano Buying Guide: The Ultimate Quick Reference to the Great Wines of Italy
(with David Lynch)

Vino Italiano: The Regional Wines of Italy
(with David Lynch)

Also by Tanya Bastianich Manuali

Lidia's Commonsense Italian Cooking (with Lidia Bastianich)

Lidia's Favorite Recipes (with Lidia Bastianich)

Lidia's Italy in America (with Lidia Bastianich)

Lidia Cooks from the Heart of Italy (with Lidia Bastianich)

Lidia's Italy (with Lidia Bastianich)

Reflections of the Breast: Breast Cancer in Art Through the Ages
(with Francis Arena)

Healthy Pasta

Healthy Pasta

The Sexy, Skinny, and Smart Way
to Eat Your Favorite Food

Joseph Bastianich and
Tanya Bastianich Manuali, PhD

Alfred A. Knopf New York 2015

This Is a Borzoi Book
Published by Alfred A. Knopf

www.aaknopf.com

Knopf, Borzoi Books, and the colophon are registered trademarks of
Penguin Random House LLC.

Library of Congress Cataloging-in-Publication Data
Bastianich, Joseph, author.
Healthy pasta : the sexy, skinny, and smart way to eat your favorite food / by Joseph Bastianich
and Tanya Bastianich Manuali.—First edition.
pages   cm
ISBN 978-0-385-35224-6 (hardcover)—ISBN 978-0-385-35225-3 (eBook)
1. Cooking (Pasta)   2. Cooking, Italian.   I. Manuali, Tanya Bastianich, author.
II. Title.
TX809.M17B376 2015   641.82'2—dc23   2014025460

Jacket photographs by Steve Giralt
Jacket design by Kelly Blair

Manufactured in the United States of America
First Edition

This book is dedicated to our Nonna Erminia, who cooked many plates
of pasta for us, all the while watching us while our mother was busy
at work. No one can beat her at growing a bountiful garden or quickly
throwing a house slipper to hit you with if you're misbehaving.
She is the root of our family, and her wisdom and love are endless.

Thank you, Nonni.

Contents

Olio/Olive Oil

Pomodoro/Tomato

Carne/Meats

Pesto

Pesce/Fish

Pasta in Modi Diversi / Pasta Done Different Ways

Healthy Pasta

Introduction

Joe It's no secret that Lidia Bastianich, the fairy godmother of pasta, is our mother. Lunch was never a simple sandwich with deli meat, and dinner could never be just one plate on the place setting. There was always a first course of pasta or soup and then a main course with salad, loads of vegetables, and usually fish, but sometimes meat. Growing up in her traditional Italian household was mostly a blessing, although sometimes the constant push to finish everything on the plate led to a bit of overeating. The upside of course was all the delicious food, having her feed armies of friends, and the fabulous kitchen aromas that always greeted us upon our returning home.

Tanya Mom always wanted us to get "an American job"—become a doctor or lawyer or something similar. The restaurant business, with its long hours and low profit margins, was the business of immigrants. So we both did something different for a while. Joe worked on Wall Street and I went into teaching, but the restaurant industry gets under your skin. Once you have experienced the nightly adrenaline of a restaurant pulsating with customers and the pressure of having to provide great service and a great experience for those customers, and then you get to fall back at the end of the night with a sigh of relief, it is very difficult to go back to any other kind of life.

The business of running restaurants in New York City and across the country, producing food shows for television, and writing cookbooks does not keep us far from fabulous food. Both of our daily routines vary from tasting new menu items to testing and tasting the dishes for a new cookbook or snacking on the spoils of a TV segment. All of it adds up to extra food and extra eating. It is difficult to control and most of the time it's a professional necessity, so we literally *can't* control it.

Joe But I got to the point where something had to change. I made a conscious effort to work out. Equally important, I realized I had to modify my eating habits. Ironically enough, though, it was my love of pasta that played a major role in helping me attain my fitness goals. I began to look at food—especially pasta—as fuel for my athletic ambitions. What began as a 10K run eventually became a marathon. Marathons became triathlons, and in 2011, I had the privilege of competing in the Kona IRONMAN world triathlon championships—and it was my daily habit of eating healthy pasta dishes that helped me get there. Once running became an integral part of my daily life, I had to find a way to make the foods I loved to eat fit my new active lifestyle, and pasta was numero uno on the list.

Change isn't always easy. But what we both learned was that great food experiences can also be healthy. In many ways, delicious food is even *more* delicious when it's healthy. Pasta in particular, an Italian favorite and something we could not live without, can most definitely be healthy. As a result, we've been able to eat it more regularly and enjoy a greater variety. Pasta is almost an obsession with our family (as it is with many families, whether Italian or not). So once we began developing healthier pasta recipes—and learned many simple tricks to make favorite recipes healthier—our obsession grew. And eating pasta became more fun because we could do it without any guilt.

Tanya Don't misunderstand the purpose of this book. Eating pasta seven days a week—and eating large portions—will never allow you to have a fully balanced diet or to lose weight. This book is not meant to be a fad diet or any miracle cure for weight problems. We did not set out to write *Lose 200 Pounds in Two Weeks by Eating Pasta!* We believe this book is a lot better than any fad diet because its effects are meant to be long lasting. It is meant to be a way to improve your eating, your health, and your life over the long haul. We know this can be done if you use the right ingredients and the right kinds of pasta, limit your portion sizes, and use many of the tricks of the trade—techniques that are easy and that we know will work because we've learned them over our two lifetimes spent around food.

Pasta has been saddled with a bad rap for far too long. The low-carb/no-carb diet craze ultimately instilled in many of us a belief that partaking of our beloved lasagna and spaghetti is a surefire path to a fat physique and a depressing result on our next visit to the doctor—and this just isn't true! Eating pasta can be beneficial to our health. It is also satisfying, economical, and should be a staple in every kitchen. Deprivation in any form almost guarantees failure. Instead of giving pasta up, we spent a lot of time finding other answers—smaller portions, for example. Another idea is to prepare your pasta simply with just a few healthy ingredients—vegetables, lean meats, and fish, dressed with olive oil.

A crucial part of the cooking process is the ingredients you choose. We all love cheese and we would never write a cookbook that eliminates cheese as a pairing with pasta. But there are cheeses that contain less fat. And did you know that peeled tomatoes have less sodium, which means they taste fresher? Throughout this book, we show you ways to add flavor to a dish that will also reduce the calories. So it boils down, no pun intended, to choosing high-quality pasta, ingredients that pack a punch of flavor without loads of calories, and cooking techniques that maximize the flavors without adding fats.

Over the years we have modified how we cook at home for our families. Kids are very active and need good food fuel. Because we are always busy with work, dinner solutions need to be quick and enjoyable. All kids love pasta, so pasta it is, but not just the starch alone; there are more vegetables incorporated. We use tomato- and olive oil–based sauces and add protein-rich ingredients—often in the same or even greater ratio to the pasta in each dish. The pasta has become a vehicle by which to serve vegetables, meat, and fish. Most sauces can be made ahead of time and then just reheated and served with pasta for dinner that night. Varying the shapes is also fun for the family. Kids like to see something a bit different every night on their dinner plates. And, as you'll see, some shapes are better for certain kinds of sauces and some shapes can even be healthier than others.

For this book, we have chosen to start with one 1-pound package of pasta per recipe and to use the whole package. Using this amount of pasta you can either feed six people or have a little bit left over to bring to work or send to school for lunch. While it is very un-Italian to eat cold pasta the next day, it is preferable to wasting food and it can be quite good that way—different tasting from when it's just cooked. Using the whole package of pasta also means that you won't have any of the annoying boxes in the pantry that are only partially full. Six portions— which is 75 grams per person—was our starting point. That comes to, just from the pasta alone, 250 calories per portion. Our goal was to have each recipe be less than a total of 500 calories per serving—so that left us with just under an extra 250 calories to create tasty, healthy sauces. *We are proud of the fact that this book gives you guidelines for exploring healthier alternatives without compromising flavor and that every recipe serving is under 500 calories.*

Quality is the key to successful pasta. Everyone knows by now that dry pasta should be cooked al dente. The reason why is less well known. Italians eat their pasta *al dente*—which means "to the tooth"; practically, it means removing pasta from the water when it's still chewy enough to have some real texture and bite to it. This is a matter of preference, but there are also health benefits to cooking pasta al dente. A pasta with bite means you have to chew more, and chewing stimulates your digestive enzymes. More chewing also means a longer and slower eating time, which allows the body to feel satiated. Don't you find that when you eat with family and friends—rather than eating alone—your food somehow tastes better? That's because good conversations around the dinner table also translate to a slower eating time, which allows your brain to send the signal that you are full before you've eaten too much. So chew your al dente pasta slowly. All those times your mother told you to slow down and chew your food, she knew what she was talking about! Also, overcooked pasta has absorbed more water in the cooking process, as

opposed to al dente pasta, which still has the potential to absorb digestive liquid in the stomach and therefore digest faster. Pasta cooked al dente has a lower glycemic index than overcooked pasta, so it has less impact on your blood sugar, which helps prevent cravings and provides a steadier supply of energy.

High-quality pasta is important. High-quality pasta will be made of durum wheat and the better the wheat quality, the higher the protein content in the pasta. The higher the protein percentage, the more bite the pasta has and the healthier it is. Durum wheat is the hardest wheat, and when milled, it breaks down to coarse particles, called semolina, which have an intense yellow color and nutty taste. When mixed with water and properly dried, durum wheat pasta has a great stability, which helps prevent it from being overcooked, if proper cooking instructions are followed. In 1967 in Italy, a law decreed that pasta could be made only from durum wheat, assuring that only the finest pasta would be produced there. Cheaper pasta on the shelves is not made from durum wheat and will mush up during the cooking process and be low in protein. You don't have to buy expensive gourmet pasta, although for a special occasion some of the fancier cuts of pasta are nice. But the few extra cents or the extra dollar you spend to buy a package of pasta with a high protein content really pays off in flavor and health benefits. It bakes down to the old adage: You get what you pay for.

Ingredients that burst with flavor are also an essential part of these dishes. Much can be done with simple ingredients such as capers, olives, anchovies, and sun-dried tomatoes. All these ingredients can be purchased either soaked in oil or cured in brine or water. When possible, stay away from the oil-cured ingredients because they have absorbed the oil, adding quite a bit of fat and calories. You can buy sun-dried tomatoes and rehydrate them in water, and then use the flavorful water as part of the recipe. You can purchase capers, artichokes, and olives in brine. Not only are these healthier, they are also less costly. When handled judiciously and with the proper techniques, tasty ingredients such as pork fats and cheeses will help you to obtain maximum flavor with minimum caloric impact.

We limit the amount of olive oil in these recipes, so use good olive oil. Extra-virgin olive oil for cooking is great. You don't have to buy expensive olive oil that is meant to be used as a raw condiment or drizzled on a finished dish. That would be overkill as well as unnecessarily costly. But do use high-quality extra-virgin olive oil meant for cooking. The better the ingredients you put in, the more flavor you get out. Many recipes call for canned tomatoes, and we suggest using Italian plum tomatoes, preferably San Marzano, because they have fewer seeds and thicker skin, and are sweeter and less acidic.

So start with a high-quality pasta and then build the flavors of your healthy dish with fresh vegetables, lean proteins, and complementary ingredients that deliver a lot of flavor in small quantities. Simple changes can make a big difference. For example, if you are lactose intolerant or just want to avoid the extra fat of cheese, you can toast bread crumbs and crushed almonds in olive oil and use the mixture to finish a dish instead of grated cheese. Oftentimes our recipes use low-fat cheeses, and it is difficult to really tell the difference; anything they might lack in flavor is compensated for by other flavor-rich ingredients. We want to teach you how to substitute or augment vegetables, and to add some extra kick with a bit more peperoncino (red pepper flakes) or a few extra capers; whatever your taste buds desire is okay, as long as you can satisfy them with low-calorie cooking techniques and flavorful low-fat ingredients.

There are cooking techniques that afford the healthy cook many alternatives to sautéing ingredients in the traditional manner. Steaming, boiling, roasting, poaching, and baking are all methods of cooking employed to make sauces with less fat that will dress pasta. Many vegetables, such as cherry tomatoes, eggplants, zucchini, or squash, intensify in flavor when baked, and if you bake them on a parchment sheet, you need no additional fat, such as butter or oil. How you cook the sauce and pasta are just as important as the quantity of each ingredient. In traditional-style cooking, most pasta sauces begin with sautéing sliced or chopped onions and/or garlic in olive oil. Recipes often call for sautéing the onion or garlic until golden or slightly browned. If the first step is sautéing directly in oil, the onion or garlic absorbs more olive oil, which is not necessarily unhealthy for you in the right quantity, but it is caloric. You can start the base for these sauces by making the onion sweat in water first so that it wilts a bit, adding some extra-virgin olive oil once it is softened. This limits the quantity of olive oil without limiting the taste. This same cooking technique can be used with vegetables that are in our sauces. Toward the end of cooking your sauce, you can always use a ladle full of pasta water to make the sauce a bit thinner to better dress the pasta. Water is the perfect calorie-free ingredient.

Al dente pasta has a more lively or viscose interaction with the sauce you serve with it. Pasta dishes often call for a specific shape of pasta; believe it or not, there are 320 recorded shapes of pasta. There is usually a clear reason for pairing a specific pasta shape with a sauce. The marriage between a pasta shape and a sauce shows how well they interplay with each other. A sauce with peas goes well with rigatoni, in which the peas can hide and then burst into your mouth as you take a steaming-hot bite. Oftentimes the pairing of pasta and sauce is a regional preference. Grandmas in Puglia have been using orecchiette with a fava bean sauce for hundreds of years. Some pasta shapes are similar: Orecchiette, shells, and pipette all have small depressions or nooks where sauce with pieces of vegetables could lodge, the pasta literally catching dollops of the sauce. However, self-expression and freedom should not be discounted in the kitchen, so you should also feel free to mix it up.

Although the recipes in this book call mostly for durum wheat pasta, here, too, as with the pasta shapes, you can make choices. Feel free to choose pasta made from different grains. Buckwheat, whole wheat, barley, lentil, flaxseed, amaranth, brown rice, kamut, quinoa, corn, and spelt pasta are all terrific choices, and some are gluten free. Sometimes several grains are milled and mixed together to make pasta. These alternative grain choices create pasta that is high in fiber, each type having a unique flavor and nutritional benefits. The cooking process of these different whole grain pastas requires some special attention, as their texture changes quickly if they are over- or undercooked. This is particularly true with gluten-free pasta, which disintegrates rather easily, lacking the gluten—a protein found in wheat, kamut, spelt, barley, and rye—that holds other pasta together. At some of our restaurants, such as Del Posto and Felidia, the chefs serve delicious gluten-free pasta that you would be hard-pressed to identify as gluten-free. While other establishments find it difficult or cost-prohibitive, more and more places are offering gluten-free alternatives. Gluten-free pasta can be used for almost any recipe in this book in the same measurement as specified in the recipe. The calories may vary slightly depending on the brand of pasta used. When choosing whole grain pasta, the calorie count of the recipes will vary, so be sure to look up the calorie count for the 75 grams per portion of the specific pasta type with which you are cooking. All dry durum wheat pasta (without egg), regardless of its shape, is about 250 calories per 75-gram portion, and all the better major brands of dry pasta have about the same calorie count. Gnocchi or dry pasta that has egg (such as pappardelle) has slightly more calories per serving, as do pasta shapes that are not made from durum wheat flour. But have fun with your pasta, and change it up by choosing different shapes that fit well with the sauce you are cooking. And trying different grain pastas, you might find that you prefer the nutty flavor of whole wheat pasta when paired with a flavorful healthy sauce.

Healthy pasta dishes are not just about good ingredients and savvy cooking techniques, however. Even if you cook healthy pasta recipes, simply eating too big a portion will detract from all the benefits you've obtained (that applies to any dish you're digging in to!). The average box or package of pasta is about 450 grams or 16 ounces, and the proper portion of uncooked pasta is about 75 grams per person, making a box the perfect meal for six people. Pasta is about sating your body and mind. Cooked properly, pasta and its sauces make for a wonderful eating experience that can also be good for you. Meals should not be about negation or depriving yourself, but rather about feeling good and giving your body the proper fuel and nutrients it needs.

The National Pasta Association found that 77 percent of Americans eat pasta at least once a week. That meal should be a joyous and satisfying one—even for your waistline. Our goal is to give you healthy, flavorful options so that you can enjoy eating pasta as much as we do. This book has all the right recipes to do just that. Because who can resist a piping-hot bowl of pasta, and why should you have to?

Get Your Grain On

TYPES OF PASTA

Whole wheat pasta is made from grinding up the whole grain, and whole wheat flour tends to be a bit heavier than traditional flour. The pasta made from it is a darker brown and has a bold, nutty taste. Take care in cooking whole wheat pastas so that the pasta remains al dente. There are 172 calories and 7.5 grams of protein in 1 cup of whole wheat pasta.

Kamut is an ancient wheat, a long grain with a brown cover. Kamut pasta is made with whole wheat and does contain gluten. It has a very soft flavor. One cup of kamut pasta has about 210 calories and 10 grams of protein.

Barley pasta is heart healthy—an excellent source of fiber and antioxidants. Made from the grain that is known for crafting flavorful beers, its rich flavor is great for almost any sauce. The outer coat of the barley is removed before milling for flour. One cup of barley pasta is about 193 calories and contains 3.5 grams of protein.

Flaxseed pasta is made of milled flaxseed and has a nutty, rich flavor. In the grinding of the seed, usually the germ, bran, and natural oils are fully preserved, providing many health benefits. Often, ground flaxseed is mixed into the flour of whole wheat pasta or buckwheat pasta. One cup of flaxseed pasta has about 215 calories and 8 grams of protein.

Spelt pasta is loaded with niacin, often associated with lowering cholesterol, and is therefore a heart-healthy choice. Spelt pasta, made from the flour of a grain used since ancient times, is rich in color and taste. It is high in protein and gluten. One cup of spelt pasta is about 190 calories and 8 grams of protein.

Jerusalem artichoke flour pasta naturally contains inulin, which causes a beneficial bacteria to grow in the digestive track, possibly lowering blood pressure and cholesterol. This pasta has a unique nutty flavor and aids digestion. Jerusalem artichoke flour alone would be gluten free; however, the pasta is almost always made with a blend of flour that includes durum wheat flour, which is not gluten free. A one-cup serving of Jerusalem artichoke pasta is about 200 calories and 7 grams of protein.

GLUTEN-FREE GRAINS

Brown rice pasta is made from ground whole brown rice. It has a very soft flavor and a smoother texture than whole wheat pasta, and it needs to be cooked a bit longer. One cup of brown rice pasta has about 210 calories and 4 grams of protein.

Quinoa, a grass plant from South America, is incredibly popular these days. It is not really a grain, but it is just as nutritionally rich. The small quinoa bead, resembling couscous, is ground into flour and then used to make pasta. Vegetarians are partial to quinoa because it is a complete protein. A complete protein contains an adequate amount of all the essential amino acids. One cup of quinoa is about 205 calories and 4 grams of protein.

Corn pasta is a whole grain pasta made of ground corn flour. It tends to cook a bit softer than other types of pasta, so watch it closely in the cooking process. One cup of corn pasta is about 203 calories and 4 grams of protein.

Buckwheat pasta has a much softer texture than many pastas. Buckwheat, a complete protein like quinoa, is really a grass, not a grain, and the seeds are ground into flour that produces a dark brown pasta noodle that has a nutty flavor. Buckwheat noodles are also known as soba noodles in Japanese cuisine. One cup of buckwheat pasta is about 200 calories and contains 6 grams of protein.

Amaranth is a tall plant with broad leaves, and it produces many seeds. Amaranth pasta is very high in protein, about 14 percent. The color is a bit lighter brown than whole wheat pasta. It has about 250 calories per cup and 9 grams of protein.

Lentil pasta is made from ground-up lentils, which are the seeds of a legume species. Lentils are higher in protein than beef, very low in fat, and high in fiber, potassium, and iron. It is more difficult to give a straightforward count for calories or protein because lentil flour is usually mixed with durum flour to make the pasta dough, and the calories and protein would really depend on the percentage of each flour used.

Chickpea flour works best when used to make fresh pasta, although often a bit of durum flour is needed to make the dough come together. Dried chickpea pasta that is completely gluten free is also available. The pasta is rich and a bit sweet in flavor. Chickpea pasta has about 280 calories per cup and 12 grams of protein.

Of course, there are also other millet flours, nut flours, grain flours, and legume flours that can be used individually or blended together to make pasta. Much of the process involves finding the right flour to provide the proper dough consistency without being too dry or too wet, or falling apart during the cooking process.

Fresh Pasta

If you have a pasta machine, you can use it here. Cut the dough into four pieces and roll each piece through to the next to last setting. For simple tagliatelle or pappardelle, though, we find it easier and less time consuming to roll and cut by hand, as directed below.

CALORIES PER SERVING:
209

2 cups all-purpose flour, plus more for rolling

1 large egg, cold

2 large egg whites, cold

2 tablespoons extra-virgin olive oil

1. Put the flour in the work bowl of a food processor and pulse once or twice to aerate it. In a spouted measuring cup, beat together the egg, egg whites, olive oil, and 3 tablespoons cold water.

2. With the machine running, pour the egg mixture through the feed tube. Process until the dough comes together in a ball around the blade. If the dough doesn't form a ball after about 15 seconds, add a tablespoon or so more flour (if it's too loose and sticky to form a ball) or water (if the dough is too crumbly to form a ball) to get to the right consistency. Once the dough forms a ball, process until the dough is smooth and springy, about 20 seconds more. Dump the dough onto a floured counter and knead a few times just to bring it together. Wrap the dough in plastic wrap and let rest at room temperature for 30 minutes. (The dough can also be made earlier in the day and refrigerated, but return the dough to room temperature before rolling.)

3. To roll, lightly dust the counter with flour. Cut the dough into four pieces, keeping the other pieces covered as you work. Pat one piece into a rectangle. Working from the center of the dough, roll up and down and left and right, occasionally flipping and flouring the dough. Once the dough is thin, you can gently rest the rolling pin in the center to anchor the dough and lightly tug it to make a rectangle 18 by 10 inches, give or take. If your dough isn't a perfect rectangle, it's okay. You'll know if it's thin enough when you can see your hand through it when you place it under the dough.

4. To cut the pasta, dust the strip with flour again. Roll the long ends of the sheet of dough up to meet in the middle, like a jelly roll. Cut crosswise through the strip to the desired thickness (1½ inches thick for pappardelle, ½ inch for tagliatelle). To unfurl the strip, slide the back of your

(continued on next page)

knife (the side opposite the blade) under the pasta so that it runs along the crease where the two rolled-up sides meet. Lift the knife up with the back of the blade facing up and the pasta will unfurl down along both sides of the knife with one or two shakes. (Or simply unfurl the pasta with your fingers.) Form the pasta into two or three loose nests and mound on a floured sheet pan. Repeat with the remaining pieces of dough. The pasta can be made several hours ahead and left at room temperature, uncovered.

5. To cook the pasta, bring a large pot of salted water to a boil. The fresh pasta will cook much more quickly than dried. Taste a strand for doneness about 3 minutes after it floats in the cooking water.

SERVES 6

CHICKPEA VARIATION: Substitute 1 cup chickpea flour for 1 cup all-purpose flour. Depending on the age and dryness of the flour, the amount of water you will use will vary. Begin with 2 tablespoons.

CALORIES PER SERVING: 207

WHOLE WHEAT VARIATION: Substitute 1 cup whole wheat flour for 1 cup of the all-purpose. You may use slightly more water with this one, but start with 3 tablespoons. Process an additional 10 to 15 seconds to get the correct smooth and silky texture.

CALORIES PER SERVING: 193

Gluten-Free Pasta

We used King Arthur brand multipurpose gluten-free flour to make this pasta. Calories will vary based on what brand or mix of gluten-free flour you chose. The amount of liquid the flour absorbs may vary too, so ¼ cup is just a guideline. Because there's no gluten to stretch the pasta, you need to roll the dough slightly thicker than the other fresh pastas in this book and cut it into shorter strands so that it doesn't fall apart when you cook it. Xanthan gum is available at baking-supply stores and in some grocery stores (in the baking/flour section) and is used to imitate gluten, replacing some of the stretching qualities of pasta made with wheat flour.

CALORIES: ABOUT 250

2 cups gluten-free flour, plus more for rolling

2 teaspoons xanthan gum

2 large eggs

2 large egg whites

1 tablespoon extra-virgin olive oil

½ teaspoon kosher salt

1. In the work bowl of a food processor, combine the flour and xanthan gum. Pulse just to combine. In a spouted measuring cup, mix the eggs, egg whites, olive oil, salt, and ¼ cup cold water until smooth. With the machine running, pour the egg mixture through the feed tube. Process until the dough comes together and is no longer crumbly, 20 to 30 seconds. (It won't come together in a ball like wheat pasta, but it will come together in several large chunks.) If the dough is too crumbly, add more water, a tablespoon at a time, until it clumps together. If it's too sticky, add more gluten-free flour, a tablespoon at a time.

2. Dump the dough on the counter and knead until it comes together in a ball. Flatten into a disk and cover in plastic wrap. Let rest at room temperature for 30 minutes.

3. When you are ready to roll, dust your work surface with gluten-free flour. Cut the dough into 4 pieces and roll the first one about ⅛ inch thick or into an 8 by 10-inch rectangle, give or take. With a pizza cutter, trim any crumbly edges from the pasta and cut it in half through the length, then into ½-inch noodles. Dust with flour and rest on floured sheet pans while you roll and cut the other pieces.

4. To cook the pasta, bring a large pot of salted water to a boil. The fresh pasta will cook much more quickly than dried, but it will take a bit longer than wheat pasta because it is cut thicker. Taste a strand for doneness about 4 minutes after it floats in the cooking water. The cooking time can vary based on the type of gluten-free flour used, so you should check often and early for doneness when cooking your pasta.

SERVES 6

Verdure

Vegetables

Pappardelle with Mushrooms

Dried pappardelle is made with eggs and is a little higher in calories than regular dried pasta, so we've cut down on the olive oil here. Finishing the dish with just a little cream results in a lush and creamy pasta that's still under 500 calories.

CALORIES PER SERVING:
427

2 tablespoons extra-virgin olive oil

1½ pounds thinly sliced mixed mushrooms (such as button, cremini, shiitake, oyster, chanterelle, or porcini) (about 10 cups)

Kosher salt and freshly ground black pepper

1 large shallot, chopped (about ⅓ cup)

2 teaspoons fresh thyme leaves, chopped

2 tablespoons tomato paste

½ cup dry white wine

1 pound dried egg pappardelle

¼ cup heavy cream

½ cup fresh Italian parsley leaves, chopped

⅓ cup freshly grated Grana Padano

1. Bring a large pot of salted water to a boil. In a large skillet over high heat, add the olive oil. When the skillet is very hot, add the mushrooms. Let sit for a minute or two, without stirring, until browned. Stir and brown the other side. Cook and stir until the mushrooms are tender and no liquid from the mushrooms remains in the pan, about 8 minutes. Season with salt and pepper.

2. Reduce the heat to medium, add the shallots and thyme, and cook until the shallots are softened, about 4 minutes. Make a space in the pan and add the tomato paste. Let toast for a minute or two, then stir it into the mushroom mixture. Increase the heat to high, pour in the white wine, and let boil until reduced to a glaze, about 1 minute. Ladle in 1 cup pasta cooking water and add the cream. Simmer until the sauce is slightly thickened, about 6 minutes.

3. Meanwhile, add the pappardelle to the boiling water (be careful, pappardelle cook faster than other pastas). When the pasta is al dente, remove it with tongs and add directly to the sauce, reserving the pasta water. Add the parsley and toss to coat the pasta in the sauce, adding a splash of pasta water if the pasta seems dry. Remove the skillet from the heat and sprinkle with the grated Grana Padano, toss, and serve.

SERVES 6

Rigatoni Boscaiola

To get the proper color (and therefore flavor) on the mushrooms that are the base of this sauce, it's important to put them in a hot pan and let them sit until they take on color. If you stir too much at the beginning, the mushrooms will release their water before browning and they'll steam instead of sauté. A traditional boscaiola sauce has a lot more cream added at the end, but a few tablespoons really go a long way, and this dish is flavorful enough as it is.

CALORIES PER SERVING:
446

2 tablespoons extra-virgin olive oil

12 ounces sliced mixed mushrooms (such as button, cremini, shiitake, oyster, chanterelle, or porcini) (about 5 cups)

1 medium onion, sliced (about 1 cup)

1 small carrot, chopped (about ½ cup)

1 celery stalk, chopped (about ½ cup)

8 fresh sage leaves, chopped

Kosher salt and freshly ground black pepper

1 (28-ounce) can whole San Marzano tomatoes, crushed by hand

3 tablespoons heavy cream

1 cup frozen peas, thawed

1 pound rigatoni

½ cup freshly grated Grana Padano

1. Bring a large pot of salted water to a boil for pasta. In a large skillet over medium-high heat, add the olive oil. When the oil is hot, add the mushrooms and let cook, without stirring, until browned, about 2 minutes. Stir and continue to cook until the mushrooms are golden and no liquid remains in the pan, about 6 minutes.

2. Reduce the heat to medium and add the onion, carrot, celery, and sage and season with salt and pepper. Cook until the onion is wilted, about 5 minutes. Add a splash of pasta cooking water and simmer until the vegetables are tender, about 4 minutes more. Add the tomatoes and 1 cup pasta water. Bring to a simmer and cook until thick and flavorful, about 20 minutes.

3. Add the cream and peas and cook until the peas are tender, about 6 minutes.

4. Meanwhile, add the rigatoni to the boiling water. When the sauce is ready and the pasta is al dente, remove the pasta with a spider or small strainer and add directly to the sauce, reserving the pasta water. Toss to coat the pasta with the sauce, adding a splash of pasta water if the pasta seems dry. Remove the skillet from the heat, sprinkle with the grated Grana Padano, toss, and serve.

SERVES 6

Whole Wheat Spaghetti with Mushroom Bolognese

Just as browning the meat properly is key to maximum flavor in the traditional Bolognese, so is browning the mushrooms here, so don't skimp on this step. A nice batch of browned mushrooms will reward you with a deep, earthy flavor when the sauce is done. We chose whole wheat spaghetti, but this elegant yet robust sauce is also a great partner for fresh pasta or gluten-free pasta. Just remember that gluten-free pasta has a very specific cooking time. We use chicken broth as the cooking liquid here, but for a true vegetarian dish, you can use vegetable broth or even plain water. If you have time, trim and destem your mushrooms ahead of time. Wash the trimmings and stems well and simmer in the chicken stock for a half hour to add extra mushroom flavor to the sauce.

CALORIES PER SERVING:
481

½ ounce dried porcini mushrooms (about 1 cup)

4 cups low-sodium chicken broth

3 tablespoons extra-virgin olive oil

2½ pounds mixed mushrooms (such as button, cremini, shiitake, oyster, chanterelle, or porcini), thickly sliced

2 medium leeks, white and light green parts, sliced (about 1 cup)

2 large shallots, chopped (about ½ cup)

10 fresh sage leaves, chopped

1 tablespoon fresh thyme leaves, chopped

¼ cup tomato paste

Kosher salt and freshly ground black pepper

1. Bring a large pot of salted water to a boil for pasta. Put the dried porcini in a spouted measuring cup with 1½ cups very hot water and let soak until softened, about 10 minutes. Drain and chop, reserving the soaking liquid. Strain the soaking liquid through cheesecloth into a clean cup and set aside. Pour the chicken broth into a small saucepan and warm over low heat.

2. In a large Dutch oven over medium-high heat, add the olive oil. When the oil is hot, add about half of the mushrooms and let sit, without stirring, until browned on the bottom, about 3 minutes. Add the remaining mushrooms and stir. Let sit and brown again, then stir. Continue this process until the mushrooms are browned all over and no liquid remains in the pot, about 15 minutes in all.

3. Reduce the heat to medium. Add the leeks, shallots, sage, and thyme and cook until wilted, about 6 minutes. Make a space in the pan and add the tomato paste. Let toast a minute or two, then stir it into the mushroom mixture, add the chopped porcini, and season everything with salt and pepper. Increase the heat to medium-high and add the red wine. Boil until reduced by half, about 2 minutes. Add the porcini liquid and bay leaves. Ladle in enough chicken broth to cover the mushrooms and bring to a simmer. Cook, partially covered, adding broth as necessary to keep the mushrooms just covered until everything is tender, about 25 minutes.

¾ cup dry red wine

2 fresh bay leaves

1 pound whole wheat spaghetti

½ cup fresh Italian parsley leaves, chopped

½ cup freshly grated Grana Padano

4. Uncover and add any remaining broth to the pot. Increase the heat so the sauce is simmering rapidly. Simmer until the sauce is thick and flavorful, about 20 minutes more.

5. Meanwhile, add the spaghetti to the boiling water. When the pasta is al dente, remove it with tongs and add directly to the sauce, reserving the pasta water. Remove the bay leaves, add the parsley, and toss to coat the pasta with the sauce, adding a splash of pasta water if the pasta seems dry (this one probably won't need it). Remove the skillet from the heat, sprinkle with the grated Grana Padano, toss, and serve.

SERVES 6

Mostaccioli with Asparagus and Roasted Mushrooms

If you can't find mostaccioli, tubular pasta similar to penne but smoother, penne or ziti is a good substitute. Mushrooms can take in a lot of oil when you sauté them, so we roast them here with herbs and garlic to cut calories and add flavor.

CALORIES PER SERVING: 399

1 pound mixed mushrooms (such as button, cremini, shiitake, oyster, chanterelle, or porcini)

1 bunch medium asparagus (about 20 spears)

3 tablespoons extra-virgin olive oil

10 fresh sage leaves, chopped

1 tablespoon fresh thyme leaves, chopped

Kosher salt and freshly ground black pepper

10 garlic cloves

1 cup chopped scallions

1 pound mostaccioli

½ cup fresh Italian parsley leaves, chopped

½ cup freshly grated Grana Padano

1. Preheat the oven to 450°F with two sheet pans on the bottom rack. (If you don't have an oven large enough to fit two pans on one rack, you can put one on the top and one on the bottom and rotate halfway through the cooking time.)

2. Bring a large pot of salted water to a boil for pasta. Wipe the mushrooms clean. Discard the stems. Cut the mushrooms into large chunks. Snap off the woody bottom stems of the asparagus and peel the lower half of the remaining tender stems. Cut the asparagus on the bias to about the same length as the mostaccioli.

3. In a large bowl, toss the mushrooms with 1 tablespoon of the olive oil and half of the sage and thyme. Season with salt and pepper. Roast on one sheet pan until the mushrooms are browned and tender, 18 to 20 minutes, tossing once or twice. In the same bowl, toss the asparagus and garlic with another 1 tablespoon of the olive oil and the remaining sage and thyme. Season with salt and pepper. Roast on the second sheet pan until the asparagus is golden and tender, and the garlic is soft, about 10 minutes. Set aside both pans on the stove top to keep warm.

4. Add the mostaccioli to the boiling water. In a large skillet over medium heat, add the remaining 1 tablespoon olive oil. Add the scallions and cook until wilted, about 3 minutes. Add the roasted garlic cloves and mash with a wooden spoon. Season with salt and pepper and add 1 cup pasta water. Bring to a simmer and cook until the garlic breaks down in the sauce, about 3 minutes.

5. When the pasta is al dente, remove it with a spider or small strainer and add directly to the sauce, along with the roasted vegetables, reserving the pasta water. Add the parsley and toss to coat the pasta with the sauce, adding a splash of pasta water if the pasta seems dry. Remove the skillet from the heat, sprinkle with the grated Grana Padano, toss, and serve.

SERVES 6

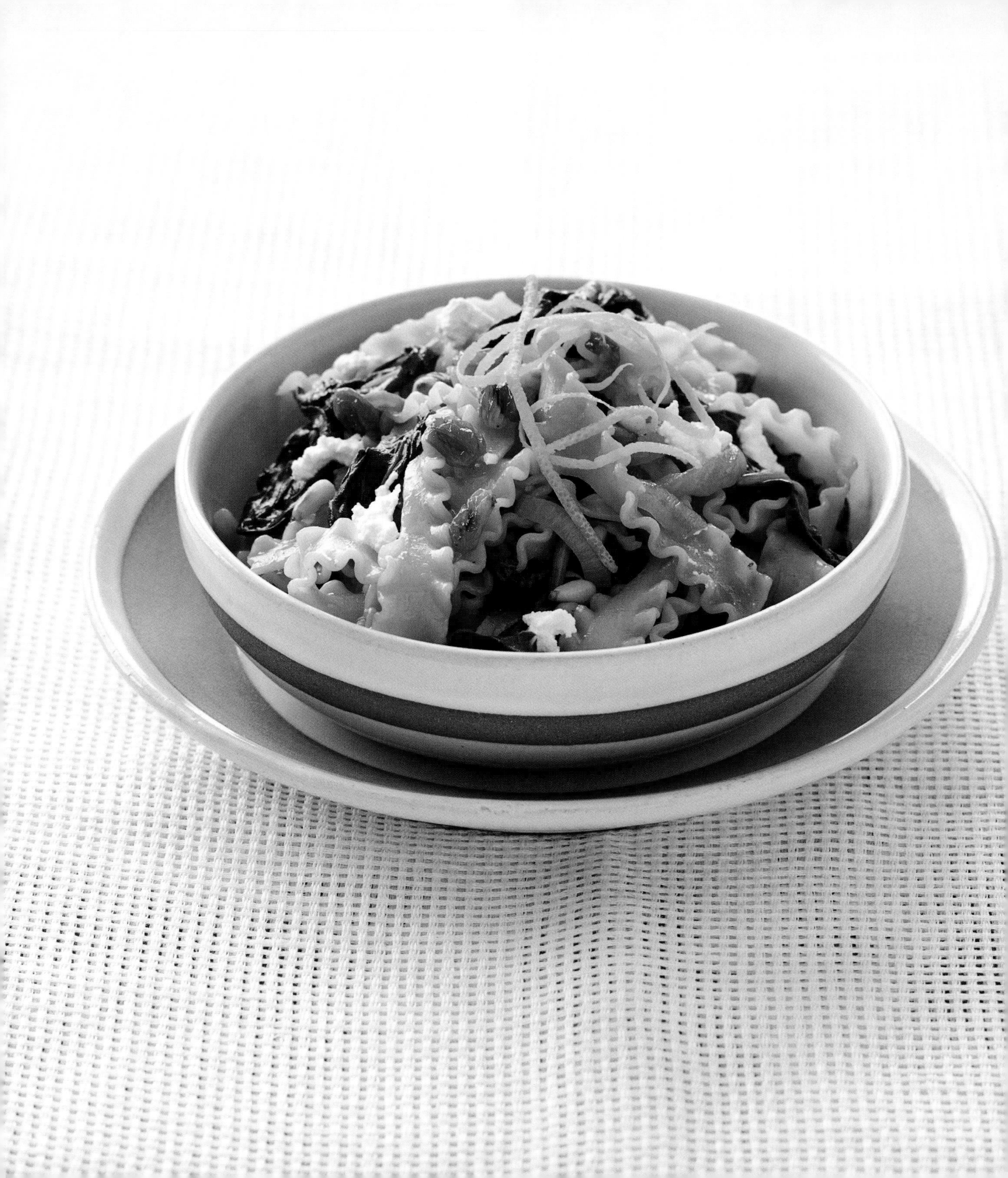

Mafalde with Spinach, Pine Nuts, and Golden Raisins

Mafalde is a long, wavy pasta. If you can't find it, substitute another wavy shape, like campanelle, or simply another long, flat shape, like fettuccine. As with almost any recipe in this book, you can also use pasta made from different grains or gluten-free pasta—just be sure to adjust the cooking time of the pasta.

CALORIES PER SERVING:
476

1 cup part-skim ricotta

¼ cup golden raisins

2 tablespoons extra-virgin olive oil

1 medium onion, sliced (about 1 cup)

12 cups packed baby spinach leaves (about 8 ounces)

Kosher salt

Crushed red pepper flakes

1 pound mafalde or fettuccine

¼ cup pine nuts, toasted and coarsely chopped

2 teaspoons orange zest

½ cup freshly grated Grana Padano

1. Put the ricotta in a small strainer lined with cheesecloth (or simply a very fine strainer without cheesecloth). Set over a bowl and let drain in the refrigerator for a couple of hours. Discard the liquid in the bottom of the bowl.

2. Bring a large pot of salted water to a boil for pasta. Put the raisins in a small bowl and ladle over enough hot pasta cooking water just to cover. Let soak for 5 minutes, drain, pat dry, and coarsely chop.

3. In a large skillet over medium heat, add the olive oil. When the oil is hot, add the onion. Cook until softened, about 5 minutes. Add the spinach and season with salt and red pepper flakes. Add 1 cup pasta water and simmer until the spinach is tender and the sauce is reduced by half, about 4 minutes.

4. Meanwhile, add the mafalde to the boiling water. When the pasta is al dente, remove it with tongs and add directly to the skillet with the spinach, reserving the pasta water. Add the raisins, pine nuts, and orange zest. Bring to a simmer and toss to coat the pasta with the sauce. Add the ricotta and stir just until it melts into the sauce, adding a splash of pasta water if the pasta seems dry. Remove the skillet from the heat, sprinkle with the grated Grana Padano, toss, and serve.

SERVES 6

Penne with Artichokes, Peas, and Ham

When selecting artichokes, look for ones that are firm and heavy for their size with tight leaves. If you rub the side with your fingers or give them a squeeze, you should hear a squeak.

CALORIES PER SERVING:
438

1 lemon, zested and cut in half

4 medium artichokes

3 tablespoons extra-virgin olive oil

2 medium leeks, white and light green parts, sliced (about 1 cup)

4 garlic cloves, thinly sliced

3 ounces ham, diced

Kosher salt and freshly ground black pepper

1 pound penne

1 cup frozen peas

½ cup fresh Italian parsley leaves, chopped

½ cup freshly grated Grana Padano

1. Bring a large pot of salted water to a boil for pasta. Fill a large bowl with cold water and squeeze the zested lemon halves into the water and add the halves. To prepare the artichokes, cut off the top third of one artichoke with a serrated knife. Pull off enough leaves to get down to the lighter colored, tender ones. Cut off and peel the stem. Trim the base, then cut the artichoke in half and scrape out the fuzzy choke with a teaspoon. Put the artichoke in the lemon water and repeat with the remaining artichokes.

2. In a large skillet over medium heat, add the olive oil. When the oil is hot, add the leeks and cook until softened, about 6 minutes. Meanwhile, remove the artichokes and stems from the water, pat dry, and thinly slice.

3. When the leeks are softened, add the garlic and ham and cook until fragrant, about 1 minute. Add the artichokes and season with salt and pepper. Add enough pasta cooking water to just cover the artichokes and sprinkle with the lemon zest. Bring to a simmer, cover, and cook until the artichokes are very tender, about 18 minutes. Uncover and boil to reduce the liquid by half, about 3 to 4 minutes.

4. Meanwhile, add the penne to the boiling water. When the pasta is about halfway cooked, add the frozen peas and cook until the pasta is al dente. Remove the penne and peas with a spider or a strainer and add directly to the sauce, reserving 1 cup pasta water. Add the parsley and toss to coat the pasta with the sauce, adding a splash of pasta water if the pasta seems dry. Remove the skillet from the heat, sprinkle with the grated Grana Padano, toss, and serve.

SERVES 6

Gnocchi with Lentils, Onions, and Spinach

We use the cooking water from the lentils as a light but flavorful broth for the base of this pasta sauce. If you want to use canned lentils, rinse and drain them and combine with the pasta water to make your sauce instead. The lentils give a richness to the sauce and readily absorb flavors from the other seasonings.

CALORIES PER SERVING:
446

½ cup brown lentils, rinsed

½ cup diced celery

½ cup diced carrot

2 garlic cloves, crushed and peeled

1 fresh bay leaf

Kosher salt

3 tablespoons extra-virgin olive oil

2 ounces pancetta, diced

1 large onion, sliced (about 1½ cups)

2 teaspoons fresh rosemary, chopped

1 tablespoon tomato paste

10 cups stemmed spinach (about 10 ounces)

Crushed red pepper flakes

1 pound dried gnocchi

½ cup freshly grated Grana Padano

I. In a medium saucepan, combine the lentils, celery, carrot, garlic, and bay leaf. Add water to cover by about 3 inches. Bring to a simmer and cook, partially covered, until the lentils are tender, 30 to 35 minutes. Season with salt and drizzle in 1 tablespoon of the olive oil. Let cool, then drain, reserving the cooking liquid.

2. Bring a large pot of salted water to a boil. In a large skillet over medium heat, add the remaining 2 tablespoons olive oil. When the oil is hot, add the pancetta and cook until the fat is rendered, about 3 minutes. Add the onion and cook until light golden, about 6 minutes. Make a space in the pan and add the rosemary and tomato paste. Let toast a minute or two, then stir the tomato paste into the onion. Add the spinach and cook until just wilted, about 3 minutes. Season with salt and red pepper flakes.

3. Add the drained lentils and 1 cup of the lentil cooking liquid (leaving the sediment at the bottom of the cup) and bring to a simmer. Meanwhile, add the gnocchi to the boiling water. When the gnocchi are al dente, drain and add to the sauce. Toss to coat the gnocchi with the sauce, adding a little more lentil cooking liquid or gnocchi water if the gnocchi seem dry. Remove the skillet from the heat, sprinkle with the grated Grana Padano, toss, and serve.

SERVES 6

Linguine with Arugula and Sun-Dried Tomatoes

This seems like a lot of arugula, but it cooks down to nothing, and its slightly bitter taste is a great match for the sweet and salty flavors of the sun-dried tomatoes and capers. Capers, especially those cured in brine instead of olive oil, pack a punch of flavor while adding almost no calories. An extra plus is that capers are a powerful antioxidant. This sauce cooks quickly. You can almost begin the sauce in the pan when you begin cooking the linguine—just soak the tomatoes first.

CALORIES PER SERVING:
413

1 cup sun-dried tomatoes (not oil packed)

¼ cup extra-virgin olive oil

5 garlic cloves, thinly sliced

2 tablespoons capers in brine, drained

1 (5-ounce) box baby arugula, about 8 cups

Kosher salt

Crushed red pepper flakes

¼ cup dry white wine

1 pound linguine

½ cup freshly grated Grana Padano

1. Bring a large pot of salted water to a boil for pasta. Put the sun-dried tomatoes in a bowl and add some of the hot pasta cooking water to cover. Let soak until softened, about 20 minutes, then drain, reserving the soaking water, and chop. (Depending on how dry your tomatoes are, you may need to add hot water halfway through the soaking time.) Measure the soaking liquid (you should have about 1 cup; if not, add pasta water to make 1 cup total).

2. In a large skillet over medium-high heat, add the olive oil. When the oil is hot, add the garlic and let it sizzle until just golden on the edges, about 1 minute. Add the chopped sun-dried tomatoes and the capers and let sizzle for a minute. Add the arugula (in batches, if necessary, letting the first batch wilt a little) and season with salt and red pepper flakes. Cook until all of the arugula is wilted, about 2 minutes. Add the white wine and bring to a boil. Add the reserved tomato soaking liquid and return to a boil. Simmer to reduce by half, about 3 minutes.

3. Meanwhile, add the linguine to the boiling water. When the sauce is reduced and the pasta is al dente, remove the pasta with tongs and add directly to the sauce, reserving the pasta water. Toss to coat the pasta with the sauce, adding up to ½ cup more pasta water if the pasta seems dry. Remove the skillet from the heat, sprinkle with the grated Grana Padano, toss, and serve.

SERVES 6

Linguine with Spinach and Lemon

Instead of cheese, this dish is finished with bread crumbs and almonds, toasted in a little olive oil, making it not only vegetarian but vegan. You can use this crispy garnish to replace the final addition of cheese in most of the simple vegetable pastas in this chapter. Grating old bread on a box grater makes larger, lighter crumbs that will crisp up wonderfully in the olive oil, but if you don't have time for that, panko bread crumbs are an acceptable substitute.

CALORIES PER SERVING:
414

3 tablespoons extra-virgin olive oil

1 (2-ounce) piece stale country bread, grated on the coarse holes of a box grater (1¼ cups crumbs)

¼ cup chopped blanched almonds

Zest and juice of 1 lemon

Kosher salt

2 cups chopped scallions

2 garlic cloves, thinly sliced

10 cups stemmed spinach (about 10 ounces)

Crushed red pepper flakes

1 pound linguine

1. Bring a large pot of salted water to a boil for pasta. In a small skillet over medium heat, add 1 tablespoon of the olive oil. Add the bread crumbs and almonds. Toss and cook until the crumbs are crisp and the almonds are toasted, 5 to 6 minutes. Scrape into a small bowl. Stir in half of the lemon zest and season with salt.

2. In a large skillet over medium-high heat, add the remaining 2 tablespoons olive oil. When the oil is hot, add the scallions and cook until wilted, about 3 minutes. Add the garlic and cook until fragrant, about 1 minute. Add the spinach and season with salt, the remaining lemon zest, and red pepper flakes. Cook and toss until the spinach is wilted, about 4 minutes. Add 1 cup pasta water and simmer until the spinach is tender, about 4 minutes.

3. Meanwhile, add the linguine to the boiling water. When the sauce is reduced and the pasta is al dente, remove the pasta with tongs and add directly to the sauce, reserving the pasta water. Toss to incorporate the pasta with the spinach and vegetables, adding a splash of pasta water if the pasta seems dry. Season with the lemon juice and toss again. Serve in warmed pasta bowls, sprinkling each serving with the almond bread crumbs.

SERVES 6

Whole Wheat Rigatoni with Leeks, Olives, and Escarole

Whole wheat pasta is a great pairing for a hearty, full-flavored sauce like this one. When working with whole wheat pasta, take extra care not to overcook it as it can go from al dente to overcooked and mushy quickly.

CALORIES PER SERVING: 423

3 tablespoons extra-virgin olive oil

2 medium leeks, white and light green parts, sliced (about 1 cup)

1 medium head escarole, washed, dried, and leaves coarsely chopped (about 6 cups)

3 garlic cloves, thinly sliced

1 tablespoon fresh thyme leaves, chopped

½ cup pitted black Italian olives (such as Gaeta), coarsely chopped (about 20)

2 tablespoons tomato paste

Kosher salt

Crushed red pepper flakes

½ cup dry white wine

1 pound whole wheat rigatoni

½ cup fresh Italian parsley leaves, chopped

½ cup freshly grated Grana Padano

1. Bring a large pot of salted water to a boil for pasta. In a large skillet over medium heat, add the olive oil. When the oil is hot, add the leeks and cook until softened, about 5 minutes. Raise the heat to medium-high and add the escarole. Cook and toss until mostly wilted, about 6 minutes. Add the garlic, thyme, and black olives and cook until fragrant, about 1 minute.

2. Make a space in the pan and add the tomato paste. Let toast for a minute until the tomato paste darkens a shade or two, then stir into the leek mixture. Season with salt and red pepper flakes. Add the white wine and bring to a simmer. Add 1 cup pasta water and let the sauce reduce by half.

3. Meanwhile, add the rigatoni to the boiling water. When the pasta is al dente and the sauce is ready, add the parsley to the sauce. Remove the pasta from the water with a spider or small strainer and add directly to the sauce, reserving the pasta water. Toss to coat the pasta with the sauce, adding a splash of pasta water if the sauce seems dry. Remove the skillet from the heat, sprinkle with the grated Grana Padano, toss, and serve.

SERVES 6

Farfalle with Romaine and Pancetta

This is great to make with a head or two of romaine that is a little past its prime—even the tough outer leaves are usable here. Pancetta, Italian salt-cured pork belly meat, adds terrific flavor, and a little bit goes a long way.

CALORIES PER SERVING:
415

2 tablespoons extra-virgin olive oil

3 ounces pancetta, diced

2 cups chopped scallions

1 large head romaine lettuce, coarsely shredded (about 12 cups)

1 tablespoon fresh thyme leaves, chopped

Kosher salt

Crushed red pepper flakes

1½ cups low-sodium chicken broth

1 teaspoon grated lemon zest

1 pound farfalle

1 cup fresh Italian parsley leaves, chopped

½ cup freshly grated Grana Padano

1. Bring a large pot of salted water to a boil for pasta. In a large skillet over medium heat, add the olive oil. When the oil is hot, add the pancetta and cook until the fat is rendered, about 4 minutes. Add the scallions and cook until wilted, about 3 minutes. Add the romaine and thyme and season with salt and red pepper flakes. Cook until the romaine is mostly wilted, about 4 minutes.

2. Add the chicken broth and lemon zest and bring to a simmer. Let the sauce simmer while you cook the pasta.

3. Add the farfalle to the boiling water. When the pasta is al dente, remove it with a spider or small strainer and add directly to the sauce, along with the parsley, reserving the pasta water. Toss to coat the pasta with the sauce, adding a splash of pasta water if the pasta seems dry. Remove the skillet from the heat, sprinkle with the grated Grana Padano, toss, and serve.

SERVES 6

Orecchiette with Swiss Chard and Ricotta Pan Sauce

This is a time when using fresh whole milk ricotta is worth the extra calories because ricotta is the star that brings together this otherwise lean dish. Caramelizing the onions over a long cooking time brings out their sweetness, which pairs well with the earthy flavor of the Swiss chard.

CALORIES PER SERVING:
467

1 large bunch Swiss chard, washed well (about 1 pound)

3 tablespoons extra-virgin olive oil

2 medium onions, sliced (about 2 cups)

3 garlic cloves, thinly sliced

2 teaspoons fresh rosemary needles, chopped

Kosher salt

Crushed red pepper flakes

1 pound orecchiette

1 cup fresh whole milk ricotta

½ cup fresh Italian parsley leaves, chopped

½ cup freshly grated Grana Padano

1. Bring a large pot of salted water to a boil for pasta. Separate the chard leaves from the stems. Coarsely chop the leaves. Trim any tough parts from the stems and discard. Finely chop the tender stems and set aside separate from the leaves.

2. In a large skillet over medium heat, add 2 tablespoons of the olive oil. When the oil is hot, add the onions and cook and stir until the onions are a deep golden color, about 15 minutes.

3. Add the chard stems and garlic and add a splash of pasta water (a couple of tablespoons) and cook until the stems are almost tender, about 10 minutes. Add the chard leaves and rosemary and season with salt and red pepper flakes. Ladle in about 2 cups pasta water and increase the heat to bring to a rapid simmer to reduce and concentrate the flavor of the sauce. Cover and cook until the chard leaves and stems are very tender, about 14 minutes.

4. Add the orecchiette to the boiling water. When the sauce is ready and the pasta is al dente, remove the pasta with a spider or small strainer and add directly to the sauce, reserving the pasta water. Reduce the heat to low and add the ricotta and parsley and drizzle with the remaining 1 tablespoon olive oil. Toss well to melt the ricotta into the sauce, adding up to 1 cup pasta water if the pasta seems dry. Remove the skillet from the heat, sprinkle with the grated Grana Padano, toss, and serve immediately.

SERVES 6

Spaghetti Primavera

The original pasta primavera from Le Cirque, while delicious, was loaded with butter, cream, and cheese. We've switched to olive oil and added just a touch of cream at the end to bring it all together. We've also streamlined the original recipe, which makes a separate tomato sauce, by combining both the tomatoes and cream in one skillet.

CALORIES PER SERVING:
421

10 asparagus spears, peeled halfway down, cut into 2-inch lengths

1½ cups trimmed and halved green beans

1 cup frozen peas

2 tablespoons extra-virgin olive oil

2 cups sliced mixed mushrooms (such as button, cremini, shiitake, oyster, chanterelle, or porcini)

1 cup diced zucchini

3 plum tomatoes, seeded and diced (1½ cups)

2 garlic cloves, chopped

Kosher salt

Crushed red pepper flakes

¼ cup heavy cream

1 pound spaghetti

½ cup fresh basil leaves, chopped

½ cup freshly grated Grana Padano

1. Bring a large pot of salted water to a boil. Put the asparagus, green beans, and peas in a strainer and blanch in the hot water until crisp-tender, about 3 minutes. Remove and cool in an ice bath. Drain and pat dry.

2. In a large skillet over medium-high heat, add the olive oil. When the oil is hot, add the mushrooms and zucchini and cook without stirring until browned on the underside, about 2 minutes. Stir and brown the other side. When the mushrooms are browned and no liquid remains in the pan, add the tomatoes and garlic and cook until the garlic is fragrant and the tomatoes begin to release their juices, about 3 minutes. Season with salt and red pepper flakes. Add the cream and 1 cup pasta water and simmer until the zucchini is tender and the mixture is saucy, about 5 minutes. Add the blanched vegetables and return to a simmer.

3. Meanwhile, add the spaghetti to the boiling water. When the sauce is ready and the pasta is al dente, remove the pasta with tongs and add directly to the sauce, reserving the pasta water. Add the basil and toss to coat the pasta with the sauce, adding a splash of pasta water if the pasta seems dry. Remove the skillet from the heat, sprinkle with the grated Grana Padano, toss, and serve.

SERVES 6

Gemelli with Brussels Sprouts and Pine Nuts

In this recipe, take the time to sweat the Brussels sprouts in the oil and caramelize them—it will add a lot of flavor and virtually no calories to the sauce. We also chop the pine nuts a little to make a small amount go a long way. Save 1 tablespoon of olive oil to drizzle at the end and give a rich feel to this easy pan sauce.

CALORIES PER SERVING: 456

3 tablespoons extra-virgin olive oil

2 ounces pancetta, finely diced

1¼ pounds Brussels sprouts, halved and thinly sliced, about 6 to 7 cups

Kosher salt

Crushed red pepper flakes

1 cup chopped scallions

1 pound gemelli

½ cup fresh Italian parsley leaves, chopped

¼ cup pine nuts, toasted and coarsely chopped

6 tablespoons freshly grated Grana Padano

1. Bring a large pot of salted water to a boil. In a large skillet over medium heat, add 2 tablespoons of the olive oil and the pancetta. Cook until the fat is rendered and the pancetta is crisp, then remove to drain on a paper towel–lined plate.

2. To the oil in the pan, add the sliced Brussels sprouts and stir. Season with salt and red pepper flakes. Cook and stir until the Brussels sprouts begin to wilt and char on the edges, about 3 minutes. Add the scallions and cook until wilted, about 2 minutes. Add 2 tablespoons pasta water, cover the skillet, and cook until tender, about 3 minutes.

3. Add the gemelli to the boiling water. Uncover the skillet and increase the heat to high. Cook until any liquid in the pan has boiled away and the Brussels sprouts are caramelized on the edges, about 2 minutes. Add 1 cup pasta water and bring to a simmer. Let reduce by half while the pasta cooks.

4. When the pasta is al dente, remove it with a spider or small strainer and add directly to the sauce, reserving the pasta water. Add the reserved pancetta, the parsley, and pine nuts and drizzle with the remaining 1 tablespoon olive oil. Toss to coat the pasta in the sauce, adding a splash of pasta cooking water if the pasta seems dry. Remove the skillet from the heat, sprinkle with the grated Grana Padano, toss, and serve.

SERVES 6

Orecchiette with White Beans and Golden Onions

The small amount of balsamic vinegar in this sauce helps caramelize the onions and brings out their natural sweetness without making them cloying. Invest in a good-quality jar of anchovies imported from Italy. Just a couple of anchovies will add a deep flavor to your sauce without a lot of calories. Once the jar is opened, store in the refrigerator, making sure the anchovies are covered in olive oil, adding more as necessary.

CALORIES PER SERVING:
445

3 tablespoons extra-virgin olive oil

1 large onion, thinly sliced (about 1½ cups)

Pinch of sugar

3 anchovy fillets, packed in oil, drained

2 teaspoons fresh thyme leaves, chopped

Kosher salt

Crushed red pepper flakes

1 tablespoon balsamic vinegar

1 (15-ounce) can cannellini beans, rinsed and drained (1¾ cups)

1 pound orecchiette

1 cup fresh Italian parsley leaves, chopped

½ cup freshly grated Grana Padano

1. Bring a large pot of salted water to a boil for pasta. In a large skillet over medium heat, add 2 tablespoons of the olive oil. When the oil is hot, add the onion and pinch of sugar. Cook, stirring occasionally, until the onion is deep golden, about 18 minutes.

2. Increase the heat to medium-high and add the anchovies and thyme. Season with salt and red pepper flakes, but be careful—the anchovies are also salty. Cook and stir, breaking up the anchovies with a wooden spoon, until the anchovies dissolve, about 2 minutes. Add the vinegar and simmer to reduce it away. Add the drained beans and toss to coat in the oil. Add 1½ cups pasta water, bring to a simmer, and let cook until reduced by about half, about 4 minutes.

3. Once the sauce is simmering, add the orecchiette to the boiling water. When the sauce is ready and the pasta is al dente, remove the pasta with a spider or small strainer and add directly to the sauce, reserving the pasta water. Add the parsley and the remaining 1 tablespoon olive oil and toss to coat the pasta with the sauce, adding a splash of pasta water if the pasta seems dry. Remove the skillet from the heat, sprinkle with the grated Grana Padano, toss, and serve.

SERVES 6

Penne with Asparagus and Goat Cheese

This no-cook sauce comes together quickly. Work fast once the pasta is cooked, so the hot water and pasta melt the goat cheese and Grana Padano quickly to make a creamy sauce. There are good-quality lower-fat goat cheeses for sale. Coach Farms makes a delicious one, and if you can find it, using it will trim some fat from this dish.

CALORIES PER SERVING:
432

1 large bunch asparagus (about 30 spears)

2 tablespoons plus 2 teaspoons extra-virgin olive oil

Kosher salt and freshly ground black pepper

1 pound penne rigate

Zest of 1 lemon and juice of ½ lemon

½ cup chopped fresh chives

5 ounces fresh goat cheese

½ cup freshly grated Grana Padano

1. Preheat the oven to 450°F with a sheet pan on the lower rack.

2. Bring a large pot of salted water to a boil for pasta. Snap off the woody lower stems of the asparagus and peel the lower half of the stems that remain. Cut the asparagus on the bias into pieces about the same length as the penne. Toss the asparagus in a large bowl with 2 teaspoons of the olive oil and season with salt and pepper. Roast on the preheated sheet pan until tender, 7 to 8 minutes, depending on the thickness of the asparagus.

3. Meanwhile, add the penne to the boiling water. Warm a serving bowl with hot water and dump the water out. To the warm bowl, add the remaining 2 tablespoons olive oil, the lemon zest, lemon juice, and chives. Season with salt and pepper. Crumble in the goat cheese.

4. When the pasta is al dente, drain, reserving 1 cup pasta water. Quickly add the pasta, roasted asparagus, and ½ cup pasta water to the bowl, along with the grated Grana Padano. Toss well to make a creamy sauce. Add a splash of the pasta water if the pasta seems dry and toss again. Serve immediately.

SERVES 6

Orzo with Mint and Peas

We cook this pasta risotto style, toasting the orzo in a little olive oil first to add flavor, then finishing with chicken broth. This can be a main dish for six (and you still have room in your calories to add a little lean protein) or a side for eight or more for a chicken or lamb dish.

CALORIES PER SERVING:
417

6 to 7 cups low-sodium chicken broth

1 cup frozen peas

1½ cups sugar snap peas, trimmed and halved crosswise

1½ cups snow peas, trimmed and halved crosswise

2 tablespoons extra-virgin olive oil

1 cup chopped scallions

1 pound orzo

Kosher salt and freshly ground black pepper

Zest of 1 lemon

½ cup fresh mint leaves, chopped

2 tablespoons unsalted butter

½ cup freshly grated Grana Padano

1. Bring a large pot of salted water to a boil. In a medium saucepan, heat the chicken broth just to a simmer. Add the peas to the boiling water, let cook for 2 minutes, then add the sugar snap peas and snow peas. Cook until al dente, about 2 minutes more. Rinse and cool under cold running water, reserving the cooking water.

2. Meanwhile, in a large skillet over medium heat, add the olive oil. When the oil is hot, add the scallions and cook until wilted, about 3 minutes. Add the orzo and cook and stir until lightly toasted, about 6 minutes.

3. Add enough chicken broth just to cover the orzo and adjust the heat so that the broth is just simmering. Cook and stir, as you would risotto, until the liquid is almost absorbed. Add more broth to cover. Continue this process until the orzo is just al dente, about 16 minutes from the first addition of broth, then add the peas and one final ladle of broth, so the mixture is just a bit soupy. (If you find you don't have enough broth, use a ladle of the vegetable cooking water.)

4. Season with salt and pepper and stir in the lemon zest and mint. Remove the skillet from the heat, vigorously stir in the butter and grated Grana Padano, and serve immediately.

SERVES 6

Spicy Shells with Sweet Potatoes

Sweet potatoes are chock-full of vitamins A and C, potassium, and fiber. They add a sweetness to the sauce usually obtained by caramelizing onions in a lot of butter. Preheating the sheet pan in the oven allows you to use less oil and still get crispy, golden brown sweet potatoes because they begin searing on contact with the pan.

CALORIES PER SERVING:
452

1 pound sweet potatoes, with skin, cut into ½-inch dice

3 tablespoons extra-virgin olive oil

Kosher salt

2 ounces pancetta, diced

2 medium leeks, white and light green parts. sliced (about 1 cup)

1 jalapeño or Fresno chile, thinly sliced (leave seeds in for the most heat)

½ teaspoon ground fennel seeds

Crushed red pepper flakes

1 pound medium shell pasta

½ cup fresh Italian parsley leaves, chopped

½ cup freshly grated Grana Padano

1. Preheat the oven to 450°F with a sheet pan on the bottom rack.

2. Bring a large pot of salted water to a boil for pasta. In a large bowl, toss the sweet potatoes with 1 tablespoon of the olive oil and season with salt. Spread the sweet potatoes on the preheated sheet pan and roast until browned on the edges and tender throughout, 18 to 20 minutes, stirring once halfway through.

3. Meanwhile, in a large skillet over medium-high heat, add 1 tablespoon of the remaining olive oil. Add the pancetta and cook until the fat is rendered, about 3 minutes. Add the leeks, chile, and ground fennel and season with salt and red pepper flakes. Cook until the leeks are wilted, about 4 minutes, then add about 1 cup pasta water.

4. Once the sauce is simmering, add the shells to the boiling water. Let the sauce simmer until reduced by half, about 8 minutes, then add the roasted sweet potatoes. When the pasta is al dente, remove it with a spider or small strainer and add directly to the sauce, reserving the pasta water. Drizzle with the remaining 1 tablespoon olive oil and toss to coat the pasta with the sauce, adding a splash of pasta water if the pasta seems dry. Remove the skillet from the heat, sprinkle with the grated Grana Padano, toss, and serve immediately.

SERVES 6

Linguine with Pancetta, Peas, and Zucchini

Use a vegetable peeler to peel the zucchini lengthwise into thin ribbons, stopping when you get to the very center where it is all seeds. You can use this same technique with carrots and peel long carrot ribbons, or also choose to use half carrots and half zucchini. The zucchini (or carrots or both) sliced this way also make a light, fresh summer salad when tossed raw with lemon juice, olive oil, and fresh herbs.

CALORIES PER SERVING:
422

2 tablespoons extra-virgin olive oil

3 ounces pancetta, diced

1 cup chopped scallions

2 garlic cloves, thinly sliced

1 pound linguine

1 cup frozen peas

2 medium zucchini, peeled into ribbons (see headnote)

Kosher salt

Crushed red pepper flakes

½ cup fresh basil leaves, chopped

½ cup fresh Italian parsley leaves, chopped

½ cup freshly grated Grana Padano

1. Bring a large pot of salted water to a boil for pasta. In a large skillet over medium heat, add the olive oil. When the oil is hot, add the pancetta and cook until the fat is rendered, about 4 minutes. Add the scallions and garlic and cook until the scallions are wilted, about 3 minutes.

2. Add the linguine to the boiling water. Once the pasta is cooking, add the peas and zucchini to the skillet and season with salt and red pepper flakes. Toss until the zucchini begin to wilt, about 2 minutes. Ladle in 1 cup pasta water and simmer and reduce by half while the pasta cooks.

3. When the pasta is al dente, remove it with a spider or small strainer and add directly to the sauce, along with the basil and parsley, reserving the pasta water. Toss to coat the pasta with the sauce, adding a splash of pasta water if the pasta seems dry. Remove the skillet from the heat, sprinkle with the grated Grana Padano, toss, and serve.

SERVES 6

Campanelle with Cauliflower, Sun-Dried Tomatoes, and Garlic

Campanelle are a great choice for this dish because they cradle the bits of cauliflower and sun-dried tomato, but if you can't find them, use another shell-shape pasta. Don't throw away the tender leaves of the cauliflower—they have as much great flavor as the florets themselves and cook in the same amount of time. Cauliflower, one of the cruciferous vegetables, is an antioxidant and detoxifying, heart healthy, and important in cancer prevention. What more can we ask for?

CALORIES PER SERVING:
399

¾ cup sun-dried tomatoes (not oil packed)

2 tablespoons extra-virgin olive oil

1 large onion, sliced (about 1½ cups)

6 garlic cloves, thinly sliced

8 fresh sage leaves, chopped

1 small head cauliflower, cut into very small florets, tender leaves coarsely chopped (about 6 cups)

3 tablespoons tomato paste

Kosher salt

Crushed red pepper flakes

½ cup dry white wine

1 pound campanelle

1 cup fresh Italian parsley leaves, chopped

½ cup freshly grated Grana Padano

1. Bring a large pot of salted water to a boil for pasta. Put the sun-dried tomatoes in a bowl and add hot water to cover. Soak until softened, about 20 minutes, then drain, reserving the soaking water, and chop. (If your tomatoes are dry, add more hot water halfway through soaking.) Measure the soaking liquid (you should have about 1 cup left over; if not, add pasta water to make 1 cup total).

2. In a large skillet over medium heat, add the olive oil. Add the onion and cook until just wilted, about 5 minutes. Add the garlic and sage and cook until fragrant, about 1 minute. Add the cauliflower and increase the heat to medium-high. Toss and cook until just golden on the edges, about 5 minutes. Make a space in the pan, add the tomato paste, and, stirring in that spot, let toast and darken a shade or two, about 2 minutes. Stir into the cauliflower mixture. Season with salt and red pepper flakes.

3. Add the white wine and simmer to reduce by half, about 1 or 2 minutes. Add the tomato soaking liquid and chopped sun-dried tomatoes. Cover and cook until the cauliflower is tender, about 5 minutes. Uncover and let the liquid reduce. Then continue cooking until the cauliflower is caramelized all over, about 4 minutes.

4. Meanwhile, add the campanelle to the boiling water. When the cauliflower is ready and the pasta is al dente, add 1 cup pasta water and the parsley to the sauce and bring to a simmer. Remove the pasta with a spider or small strainer and add directly to the sauce, reserving the pasta water. Toss to coat the pasta in the sauce, adding a splash of pasta water if the pasta seems dry. Remove the skillet from the heat, sprinkle with the grated Grana Padano, toss, and serve.

SERVES 6

Ziti with Savoy Cabbage and Pancetta

A few dried porcini mushrooms add to the heartiness of this sauce, without your needing to include a lot of meat—or calories. The wrinkly leaves of savoy cabbage hold their shape well as they cook and have a slightly less sulfurous taste than green cabbage. However, if you can't find savoy cabbage, you can certainly make this dish with green cabbage. All cabbage contains sinigrin, which is known to be especially important in cancer prevention.

CALORIES PER SERVING:
474

½ ounce dried porcini mushrooms (about 1 cup)

1 tablespoon extra-virgin olive oil

4 ounces pancetta, diced

2 cups sliced leeks, white and light green parts

1 small head savoy cabbage, shredded (about 10 cups)

1 tablespoon fresh thyme leaves, chopped

Kosher salt

Crushed red pepper flakes

3 tablespoons tomato paste

½ cup dry white wine

2 fresh bay leaves

1 pound ziti

½ cup fresh Italian parsley leaves, chopped

½ cup freshly grated Grana Padano

1. Bring a large pot of salted water to a boil for pasta. Ladle 1 cup hot pasta water into a spouted measuring cup and add the porcini. Let soak until softened, about 15 minutes. Strain and reserve the soaking water. Chop the mushrooms.

2. Heat a large Dutch oven over medium heat. Add the olive oil. When the oil is hot, add the pancetta and cook until the fat is rendered, about 4 minutes. Add the leeks and cook until wilted, about 5 minutes. Add the cabbage, thyme, and ½ cup pasta water. Season with salt and red pepper flakes. Cover and let cook, stirring occasionally, until the cabbage has softened, about 18 minutes.

3. Uncover and increase the heat to medium-high to boil away any excess liquid in the pan. When everything is sizzling, make a space in the pan and add the tomato paste. Cook, stirring in that spot, until the tomato paste toasts and darkens a shade or two, about 2 minutes. Stir into the cabbage mixture. Add the white wine and bring to a simmer. Add the bay leaves and chopped porcini. Add the porcini soaking liquid and 1 cup pasta water. Adjust the heat to bring the mixture to a simmer, and cook until the cabbage is very tender, about 10 minutes.

4. Add the ziti to the boiling water. When the sauce is ready and the pasta is al dente, remove the pasta with a spider or small strainer and add directly to the sauce, reserving the pasta water. Toss to coat the pasta with the sauce and remove the bay leaves. Remove the skillet from the heat, sprinkle with the grated Grana Padano, toss, and serve.

SERVES 6

Gnocchi with Broccolini and Anchovy Sauce

All brands of gnocchi will cook slightly differently, depending on the size and how dry they are. When cooking gnocchi, make sure the water is boiling vigorously and salted prior to dropping them in. They should gently slide into the water, so as not to break. The gnocchi will sink at first, but slowly rise to the top as they continue to cook. Once they are mostly all floating on top, carefully strain them. Gnocchi are very filling, so a little goes a long way. Knowing the exact calorie count of gnocchi can be difficult depending on if the other ingredients were used in addition to or in substitution for the typical potatoes, eggs, and flour. One serving of 100 grams is about 105 calories, depending on the brand purchased, and 1 cup of gnocchi has about 5 grams of protein.

CALORIES PER SERVING:
389

2 tablespoons unsalted butter

2 medium leeks, white and light green parts, sliced (about 1 cup)

2 bunches broccolini, trimmed and cut into 2-inch pieces (about 8 cups)

Kosher salt

Crushed red pepper flakes

4 anchovy fillets

3 garlic cloves, sliced

1 cup low-sodium chicken broth

6 cups fresh or frozen gnocchi (about 24 ounces)

1 cup shredded low-moisture part-skim mozzarella

½ cup freshly grated Grana Padano

1. Preheat the broiler.

2. Bring a large pot of salted water to a boil for the gnocchi. In a large oven-proof skillet over medium heat, melt the butter. Add the leeks and cook, stirring often, until wilted but not colored, about 5 minutes. Add the broccolini and season with salt and red pepper flakes. Cook until the broccolini is bright green and the ends begin to wilt, about 3 minutes.

3. Make a space in the pan and add the anchovies and garlic. Let them sizzle for a minute, then stir to dissolve the anchovies. Add the chicken broth, cover, and simmer until the broccolini is tender, about 8 minutes.

4. Meanwhile, slide the gnocchi into the boiling water. Cook the gnocchi according to the package directions. In a small bowl, toss together the mozzarella and grated Grana Padano. When the gnocchi is cooked, remove it with a spider or small strainer and add directly to the sauce, reserving the cooking water. Toss to coat the gnocchi with the sauce, adding a splash of cooking water if the gnocchi seem dry (though this one should not be as saucy as the other recipes here). Sprinkle with one-third of the cheese mixture and stir it in. Sprinkle with the remaining cheese and broil until the cheese is browned and bubbly, about 3 minutes. Serve immediately.

SERVES 6

Linguine with Caramelized Onions and Radicchio

The sweetness of the caramelized onions balances the bitter radicchio in this simple, quick pasta dish. You can also make this with a combination of bitter greens, such as escarole or broccoli di rabe. Radicchio, part of the chicory family, aids in weight loss by being high in fiber.

CALORIES PER SERVING:
404

3 tablespoons extra-virgin olive oil

2 large heads radicchio, coarsely shredded (about 6 packed cups)

Kosher salt

Crushed red pepper flakes

2 large onions, sliced (about 3 cups)

1 tablespoon fresh thyme leaves, chopped

2 teaspoons balsamic or sherry vinegar

1 cup low-sodium chicken broth

1 pound linguine

1 cup fresh Italian parsley leaves, chopped

½ cup freshly grated Grana Padano

I. Bring a large pot of salted water to a boil for pasta. Heat a large skillet over medium-high heat. Add 1 tablespoon of the olive oil. When the oil is hot, sear the radicchio all over until browned on the edges, about 3 minutes, then remove to a plate. Season with salt and red pepper flakes.

2. Reduce the heat to medium-low and add the remaining 2 tablespoons olive oil and the onions. Toss to coat the onions in the oil and season with salt and red pepper flakes. Add the thyme and vinegar and cook until the onions are very soft and deep golden, 20 to 25 minutes. Return the radicchio to the skillet and add the chicken broth. Let the sauce simmer while you cook the pasta.

3. Add the linguine to the boiling water. When the pasta is al dente, remove it with tongs and add directly to the sauce, along with the parsley, reserving the pasta water. Toss to coat the pasta in the sauce, adding a splash of pasta water if the pasta seems dry. Remove the skillet from the heat, sprinkle with the grated Grana Padano, toss, and serve.

SERVES 6

Spaghetti with Fennel and Anchovies

This simple sauce is all about taking the time to cook down the fennel and onions until they're soft, silky, and sweet. The anchovies add a salty, savory note to balance the dish. Anchovies, part of the herring family, are not the most popular food choice and many people stay away from them, mostly because they know them as the fishy-tasting and oversalted fish in a can or jar. However, when used properly in cooking, they add tons of flavor, umami, which in the food world is almost an inexplicable under layer of flavor. When anchovies are mixed into a recipe, their single flavor is almost undetectable, but what they add to the whole dish is incomparable.

CALORIES PER SERVING:
392

3 tablespoons extra-virgin olive oil

2 small bulbs fennel, cored and sliced (about 3 cups), plus 1 cup fronds, chopped

1 large onion, sliced (about 1½ cups)

2 fresh bay leaves

6 garlic cloves, thinly sliced

6 anchovy fillets

½ teaspoon ground fennel seeds

Kosher salt

Crushed red pepper flakes

1 pound spaghetti

½ cup fresh Italian parsley leaves, chopped

¾ cup freshly grated Grana Padano

1. Bring a large pot of salted water to a boil for pasta. In a large skillet over medium heat, add the olive oil. When the oil is hot, add the sliced fennel and onions and toss to coat in the oil. Add the bay leaves and cook, stirring often until the fennel and onion are golden, about 20 minutes.

2. Add the garlic, anchovies, and ground fennel and cook, stirring, until the anchovies dissolve into the oil, about 3 minutes. Season with salt and red pepper flakes. Add 1½ cups pasta water and bring to a simmer. Cook until the sauce is reduced by half and the vegetables are very tender, about 5 minutes.

3. Meanwhile, add the spaghetti to the boiling water. When the sauce is ready, add the parsley. When the pasta is al dente, remove it with tongs and add directly to the sauce, reserving the pasta water. Toss to coat the pasta with the sauce, adding a splash of pasta water if the pasta and fennel fronds seem dry. Remove the bay leaves. Remove the skillet from the heat, sprinkle with the grated Grana Padano, toss, and serve.

SERVES 6

Olio

Olive Oil

Penne with Broccoli, Garlic, and Oil

We've added a little pancetta to this sauce, but you could easily leave it out to make it vegetarian and just add an extra tablespoon of oil. Roasting the broccoli with a little oil brings out its sweetness before you sauté it. The tanginess of Pecorino cheese goes well with this sauce, but you could also use Grana Padano if that's what you have in the house.

CALORIES PER SERVING:
470

2 small heads broccoli, trimmed into small florets, tender stems peeled and sliced ¼ inch thick (about 12 cups)

3 tablespoons extra-virgin olive oil

Kosher salt

2 ounces pancetta, diced

6 garlic cloves, thinly sliced

1 medium onion, sliced (about 1 cup)

Crushed red pepper flakes

1 pound penne

½ cup fresh Italian parsley leaves, chopped

½ cup freshly grated Pecorino Romano

1. Preheat the oven to 450°F with a sheet pan on the lower rack.

2. Bring a large pot of salted water to a boil for pasta. In a large bowl, toss the broccoli with 2 tablespoons of the olive oil and season with salt. Place the broccoli on the sheet pan and roast, tossing once, until charred on the edges and just tender, about 13 minutes. (It will cook more in the sauce.)

3. Meanwhile, in a large skillet over medium heat, add the remaining 1 tablespoon olive oil. When the oil is hot, add the pancetta and cook until the fat is rendered and the pancetta begins to crisp, about 3 minutes. Add the garlic and onion and cook until golden, about 10 minutes. Season with salt and red pepper flakes. Add 1 cup pasta cooking water, bring to a simmer, and add the roasted broccoli. Let simmer while you cook the pasta.

4. Add the penne to the boiling water. When the sauce is ready and the pasta is al dente, remove the pasta with a spider or small strainer and add directly to the sauce, along with the parsley, reserving the pasta water. Toss to coat the pasta with the sauce, adding a splash of pasta water if the pasta seems dry. Remove the skillet from the heat, sprinkle with the grated Pecorino Romano, toss, and serve.

SERVES 6

Spaghetti with Garlic and Oil

While this recipe contains more fat than some of our others, it's still relatively low in calories for an entrée that is so satisfying. The classic version of the sauce is just these ingredients (though in greater amounts), but you could also add seafood (most shellfish will do) or roasted vegetables to take this dish in another direction. Another simple variation is to add a couple sprigs of a fresh herb (sage or rosemary would work particularly well) to the oil to flavor the sauce; just pluck them out before serving.

CALORIES PER SERVING:
428

5 tablespoons extra-virgin olive oil

12 garlic cloves, thinly sliced

Kosher salt

Crushed red pepper flakes

2 cups fresh Italian parsley leaves, chopped

1 pound spaghetti

¾ cup freshly grated Grana Padano

1. Bring a large pot of salted water to a boil for pasta. Heat a large skillet over medium heat and add the olive oil. Scatter in the garlic and stir to coat in the oil. Let the garlic slowly cook in the oil until softened and very fragrant, about 6 minutes, but don't let the garlic color.

2. Once the garlic is softened, increase the heat to medium-high and let the garlic sizzle for a minute until the edges are just golden. Season with salt and red pepper flakes. Add 1½ cups pasta water and the parsley and bring to a rapid boil. Let the sauce reduce by half while you cook the pasta.

3. Add the spaghetti to the boiling water. When the sauce is ready and the pasta is al dente, remove the pasta with tongs and add directly to the sauce, reserving the pasta water. Toss well to coat the pasta with the sauce and season with salt and red pepper flakes. Let simmer a minute to steep the garlic flavor into the pasta, then remove the skillet from the heat, sprinkle with the grated Grana Padano, toss, and serve.

SERVES 6

Bucatini with Garlic, Oil, and Anchovies

This sauce is all about the anchovies, so buy high-quality jarred anchovies packed in olive oil and imported from Italy. They're larger than canned anchovies and have a richer, less salty flavor. We've gone against the tradition of no cheese with fish and added a little Grana Padano at the end because we think the combination works here, but go easy on the extra salt.

CALORIES PER SERVING:
382

3 tablespoons extra-virgin olive oil

8 garlic cloves, thinly sliced

10 imported Italian anchovies, packed in oil, drained and patted dry

2 teaspoons fresh thyme leaves, chopped

Kosher salt

Crushed red pepper flakes

1 pound bucatini

1 cup fresh Italian parsley leaves, chopped

¾ cup freshly grated Grana Padano

I. Bring a large pot of salted water to a boil for pasta. Heat a large skillet over medium heat. Add the olive oil. Scatter in the garlic and stir to coat in the oil. Let the garlic slowly cook in the oil until softened and very fragrant, about 6 minutes, but don't let the garlic color.

2. Increase the heat to medium-high and add the anchovies and thyme. Cook, stirring with a wooden spoon, until the anchovies dissolve into the oil, 2 to 3 minutes. Add 1½ cups pasta water, season with salt and red pepper flakes, and simmer to reduce by half.

3. Meanwhile, add the bucatini to the boiling water. When the sauce is ready and the pasta is al dente, stir the parsley into the sauce. Remove the pasta with tongs and add directly to the sauce, reserving the pasta water. Toss to coat the pasta in the sauce, adding a splash of pasta water if the pasta seems dry. Remove the skillet from the heat, add the grated Grana Padano, toss, and serve.

SERVES 6

Linguine with Broccoli di Rabe, Garlic, and Anchovies

A half teaspoon of crushed red pepper flakes will give this recipe a real kick, but feel free to add more or less to suit your taste. Slowly braising the broccoli di rabe removes a little of the bitterness and gives it a silky texture. We like the combination of a few bread crumbs and some grated Grana Padano to finish this dish, but you could also use just one or the other.

CALORIES PER SERVING: 406

⅓ cup panko (or homemade) bread crumbs

3 tablespoons plus 1 teaspoon extra-virgin olive oil

⅓ cup freshly grated Grana Padano

2 bunches broccoli di rabe (about 1¼ pounds)

6 garlic cloves, thinly sliced

4 anchovy fillets

Kosher salt

½ teaspoon crushed red pepper flakes, or to taste

1 pound linguine

1. Bring a large pot of salted water to a boil. In a small skillet over medium heat, toast the panko until just golden, about 3 minutes. Transfer to a small bowl and stir in 1 teaspoon of the olive oil. Let cool, then toss with the grated Grana Padano and set aside.

2. To prepare the broccoli di rabe, trim off and discard any tough or woody stems. Starting at the trimmed base end of the stalk, use a paring knife to peel the thick stems. Cut the broccoli di rabe into 2-inch lengths.

3. In a large skillet over medium heat, add the remaining 3 tablespoons olive oil. When the oil is hot, add the garlic. Cook until the garlic just begins to turn golden, about 2 minutes. Add the anchovies and cook, stirring, until they dissolve in the oil, about 2 minutes. Add the broccoli di rabe and toss to coat in the oil. Cook until the smaller leaves begin to wilt, then season with salt and the red pepper flakes. Add ½ cup pasta water. Adjust the heat so that the sauce is simmering and cover. Braise until the broccoli di rabe is very tender, about 12 minutes.

4. Uncover and raise the heat to reduce away the water and give the contents of the skillet a chance to caramelize a little, then add another ½ cup pasta water and simmer for another minute.

5. Meanwhile, add the linguine to the boiling water. When the sauce is ready and the pasta is al dente, remove the pasta with tongs and add directly to the sauce, reserving the pasta water. Toss to coat the pasta with the sauce, adding a splash of pasta water if the pasta seems dry. Remove the skillet from the heat, add half of the grated cheese mixture, and toss. Serve in warmed pasta bowls, sprinkled with the remaining cheese mixture.

SERVES 6

Fettuccine with Roasted Red Peppers, Rosemary, and Green Olives

Do not rinse your bell peppers after peeling off the charred skins; a lot of flavor is in the juices that collect while peeling. If any stray skin won't peel, just lay the peppers flat and scrape with a paring knife.

CALORIES PER SERVING:
433

3 medium red bell peppers

3 tablespoons extra-virgin olive oil

1 medium red onion, sliced (about 1 cup)

1 teaspoon chopped fresh rosemary needles

Kosher salt

Crushed red pepper flakes

¾ cup large pitted Italian green olives (such as Cerignola), slivered (about 20)

¼ cup dry white wine

1 pound fettuccine

½ cup fresh Italian parsley leaves, chopped

¼ cup almond slivers, toasted and coarsely chopped

½ cup freshly grated Grana Padano

I. Bring a large pot of salted water to a boil for pasta. Turn on the flame for two burners on the stove top and char the bell peppers on all sides, turning them frequently, 8 to 10 minutes. Put the peppers in a large bowl and cover tightly with plastic wrap. Let steam until cooled. Peel the skin from the peppers. Remove the stems and seeds and cut the peppers into ½-inch-thick slices.

2. In a large skillet over medium heat, add the olive oil. When the oil is hot, add the red onion and cook until softened, about 8 minutes. Add the sliced peppers and rosemary and cook until the peppers are tender, about 5 minutes. Season with salt and red pepper flakes. Add the olives and white wine and bring to a simmer. Add 1 cup pasta water and boil to reduce the sauce by half, about 5 minutes.

3. Meanwhile, add the fettuccine to the boiling water. When the sauce is ready and the pasta is al dente, remove the pasta with tongs and add directly to the sauce, reserving the pasta water. Add the parsley and almonds and toss to coat the pasta with the sauce, adding a splash of pasta water if the pasta seems dry. Remove the skillet from the heat, sprinkle with the grated Grana Padano, toss, and serve.

SERVES 6

Spaghetti Cacio e Pepe

Classic cacio e pepe is just butter, olive oil, pasta, and cheese. We've lightened it up by making an emulsion of pasta water, butter, and oil. Adding a little shaved cheese at the end highlights the flavor of the Pecorino without adding a lot of extra calories. If Pecorino is too strong for your taste, use half Pecorino and half Grana Padano.

The key to this dish is good-quality ingredients—great butter and olive oil and a fresh jar of peppercorns will make all the difference in the world. Because we've cut some of the calories and fat by reducing the amounts of cheese and butter, don't skimp on the seasoning. Aggressive seasoning with both pepper and salt will make the flavor in this dish pop.

CALORIES PER SERVING:
440

2 teaspoons freshly crushed coarse black peppercorns, plus more for garnish

1 pound spaghetti

3 tablespoons unsalted butter

3 tablespoons extra-virgin olive oil

¼ cup freshly grated pecorino Romano

¼ cup freshly grated Grana Padano

Kosher salt

1 (2-ounce) wedge Grana Padano or Pecorino Romano

I. Bring a large pot of salted water to a boil. In a small skillet, toast the peppercorns over medium heat until fragrant, about 1 minute. Set aside.

2. Add the spaghetti to the boiling water.

3. In a large skillet, melt 2 tablespoons of the butter in the olive oil over medium heat. When the butter has melted, remove 1½ cups pasta water from the pot and gradually whisk it into the butter, making sure the sauce is simmering rapidly to allow it to emulsify. Let the sauce simmer until it reduces to about 1 cup, 3 to 4 minutes.

4. When the pasta is al dente, remove it with tongs and add directly to the sauce, reserving the pasta water. Add the peppercorns and the remaining 1 tablespoon butter and season with salt. Toss to coat the pasta in the sauce, adding up to ½ cup more pasta water if the pasta seems dry. Remove from the heat, sprinkle with the mixed grated cheeses, and toss well. Serve in warmed pasta bowls, shaving the wedge of cheese, whichever you prefer, over each bowl with a vegetable peeler and topping with a final sprinkle of coarsely crushed peppercorns.

SERVES 6

Linguine with Caramelized Onions, Bacon, and Olives

Center-cut bacon is available in most grocery stores and has fewer calories and less fat than regular bacon, but it also has all of the flavor. We added a touch of balsamic to the onions to help them caramelize without needing to use excess oil.

CALORIES PER SERVING:
460

1 tablespoon extra-virgin olive oil

6 strips center-cut bacon, coarsely chopped

2 large onions, sliced (about 3 cups)

2 teaspoons balsamic vinegar

1 tablespoon fresh thyme leaves, chopped

2 tablespoons tomato paste

½ cup pitted black Italian olives (such as Gaeta), coarsely chopped

½ cup dry white wine

1 pound linguine

1 cup fresh Italian parsley leaves, chopped

½ cup freshly grated Grana Padano

1. Bring a large pot of salted water to a boil for pasta. In a large skillet over medium heat, add the olive oil. Add the bacon and cook until crisp, about 5 minutes. Remove to a paper towel to drain. (There should not be too much excess fat in the pan, because center cut is leaner, but if there is more than 3 tablespoons in the pan, pour off the excess.)

2. To the fat in the pan, add the onions and balsamic vinegar and stir. Cook, stirring often, until the onions are a deep golden, 20 to 25 minutes, adjusting the heat as you go if it looks like the onions are burning.

3. When the onions are caramelized, make a space in the pan and add the thyme and tomato paste. Cook, stirring the tomato paste in that spot, until it toasts and darkens a shade or two, about 2 minutes. Stir into the onions and add the olives and white wine. Bring to a boil and cook until the wine is syrupy, about 1 minute. Add 1 cup pasta water and simmer while you cook the pasta.

4. Add the linguine to the boiling water. When the sauce is ready and the pasta is al dente, stir the parsley and reserved bacon into the sauce. Remove the pasta with tongs and add directly to the sauce, reserving the pasta water. Toss to coat the pasta with the sauce, adding a splash of pasta water if the pasta seems dry. Remove the skillet from the heat, sprinkle with the grated Grana Padano, toss, and serve.

SERVES 6

Spinach Fettuccine with Poppy Seed Sauce

Because this sauce is so simple, we use chicken broth instead of the usual pasta water to add flavor. To bulk this up a bit without adding a lot of calories, you could toss in a few handfuls of baby spinach or baby kale with the poppy seeds. The dried spinach fettuccine is used here more for color than for any extra nutritional value it might provide.

CALORIES PER SERVING:
401

1½ cups low-sodium chicken broth

2 tablespoons unsalted butter

2 tablespoons extra-virgin olive oil

2 cups chopped scallions

Kosher salt and freshly ground black pepper

1 tablespoon poppy seeds

1 pound spinach fettuccine

½ cup fresh Italian parsley leaves, chopped

¾ cup freshly grated Grana Padano

1. Bring a large pot of salted water to a boil for pasta. Heat the chicken broth just to a simmer in a small saucepan.

2. In a large skillet over medium heat, melt the butter in the olive oil. When the butter is melted, add the scallions and cook until wilted, about 3 minutes. Season with salt and pepper. Add the poppy seeds and cook for 1 minute (you don't want them to burn). Increase the heat to medium-high and add the chicken broth. Simmer the sauce while you cook the pasta.

3. Add the fettuccine to the boiling water. When the sauce is ready and the pasta is al dente, remove the pasta with tongs and add directly to the sauce, reserving the pasta water. Toss to coat the pasta with the sauce, adding a splash of pasta water if the pasta seems dry. Remove the skillet from the heat, sprinkle with the parsley and grated Grana Padano, toss, and serve.

SERVES 6

Pomodoro

—

Tomato

Spaghettini with Raw Tomato and Garlic Sauce

Spaghettini is a good choice for this dish. It is so thin that the warm tomatoey juices from the sauce will soak all the way in and infuse the pasta with their flavor—but make sure to cook it very al dente. It almost goes without saying, but we'll say it anyway—don't make this sauce unless you have fresh-from-the-farmers'-market tomatoes, or ones that you've grown yourself. This is a very basic version of this sauce, but you could shave some ricotta salata over the top of the dish or add a handful of capers, olives, or anchovies to take the sauce to the next level.

CALORIES PER SERVING:
423

3 tablespoons extra-virgin olive oil

1 garlic clove, very finely chopped

2½ pounds mixed tomatoes (different colors and sizes)

2 cups fresh basil leaves, coarsely chopped or torn

Kosher salt and freshly ground black pepper

1 pound spaghettini

½ cup freshly grated Grana Padano

I. Bring a large pot of salted water to a boil for pasta. In a large serving bowl, stir together the olive oil and garlic. Let sit while you prepare the tomatoes.

2. Core the tomatoes and dice into 1-inch pieces. You'll get 6 or 7 cups. Add to the bowl along with the basil, season with salt and pepper, and toss well. Let sit at room temperature for 15 minutes to allow the tomatoes to release their juices.

3. Add the spaghettini to the boiling water. When the pasta is very al dente, remove it with tongs and add directly to the bowl with the tomatoes, reserving the pasta water. Toss well and let sit a minute or two for the tomato juices to soak into the pasta, then add a little more pasta water if the pasta seems dry. Sprinkle with the grated Grana Padano, toss, and serve.

SERVES 6

Cavatappi with Fresh Tomato and Ricotta Sauce

Straining and using the juices from the tomatoes as a base for the sauce is a great way to accentuate the tomato flavor without overcooking the sauce. Plum tomatoes are a good choice here because they're meaty and hold their shape when cooked.

CALORIES PER SERVING:
467

1½ cups part-skim ricotta

2 pounds ripe tomatoes (6 medium)

3 tablespoons extra-virgin olive oil

Kosher salt

Crushed red pepper flakes

1 pound cavatappi

1 cup chopped scallions

3 garlic cloves, thinly sliced

1 cup fresh basil leaves, chopped

½ cup freshly grated Grana Padano

1. Put the ricotta in a small strainer lined with cheesecloth (or simply a very fine strainer without cheesecloth). Set over a bowl and let drain in the refrigerator for a couple of hours. Discard the liquid in the bottom of the bowl.

2. Bring a large pot of salted water to a boil for pasta. Core and halve the tomatoes. Scoop the seeds and pulp into a strainer set over a bowl and press on the solids to extract as much juice as possible. (You should have about ¾ cup juice.) Chop the tomatoes into ½-inch pieces. Toss the tomatoes in a large bowl with 2 tablespoons of the olive oil and season with salt and red pepper flakes. Let sit for 15 minutes to release some juices.

3. Add the cavatappi to the boiling water. Meanwhile, heat a large skillet over medium-high heat. Add the remaining 1 tablespoon olive oil. When the oil is hot, add the scallions and garlic and cook until wilted, about 3 minutes. Season with salt and red pepper flakes. Add the reserved tomato juices. Bring to a simmer and cook until reduced by half, about 3 minutes. Add the tomatoes and cook until just warmed through, about 2 minutes.

4. When the pasta is al dente, remove it with a spider or small strainer and add directly to the sauce, reserving the pasta water. Add the drained ricotta and the basil and toss just until the ricotta is hot and melts into the sauce, about 1 minute. Remove the skillet from the heat, sprinkle with the grated Grana Padano, toss, and serve.

SERVES 6

Rigatoni alla Norma

An eggplant is like a sponge, notorious for soaking up oil during cooking. We toss the eggplant with a small amount of oil and roast it at high heat to keep down the calories and fat before we finish it in a simple tomato sauce. Many recipes call for salting an eggplant before cooking, but if you use the smaller, sweeter Italian eggplant with fewer seeds, salting isn't necessary—cutting down on your time and sodium as well.

CALORIES PER SERVING:
440

3 tablespoons extra-virgin olive oil

3 small Italian eggplants, cut into 1-inch cubes (about 7 cups)

Kosher salt

1 medium onion, chopped (about 1 cup)

3 garlic cloves, thinly sliced

¼ teaspoon crushed red pepper flakes

1 (28-ounce) can whole San Marzano tomatoes, crushed by hand

1 pound rigatoni

½ cup fresh basil leaves

1 (3-ounce) piece ricotta salata

1. Preheat the oven to 450°F with a sheet pan on the top rack.

2. Bring a large pot of salted water to a boil for pasta. On the preheated sheet pan, toss the eggplants with 1½ tablespoons of the olive oil and season with salt. Roast, tossing the eggplants occasionally, until they are browned and tender, about 18 minutes.

3. While the eggplants are roasting, begin the sauce. In a large skillet over medium heat, add the remaining 1½ tablespoons olive oil. When the oil is hot, add the onion. Cook and stir until the onion begins to soften, about 4 minutes. Add the garlic and cook until fragrant, about 1 minute. Increase the heat to medium-high, add a ladleful of pasta water (about ½ cup), and simmer rapidly until the onion is soft and the water has evaporated, about 5 minutes. Season with salt and the red pepper flakes. Add the tomatoes and 1½ cups pasta water, bring to a rapid simmer, and cook until slightly thickened, about 10 minutes.

4. When the sauce is ready, add the roasted eggplants to the sauce and the rigatoni to the boiling water. When the pasta is al dente, remove it with a spider or small strainer and add directly to the sauce, reserving the pasta water. Roughly tear the basil leaves right into the sauce. Toss to coat the pasta in the sauce, adding a splash of pasta water if the pasta seems dry. Serve, shaving the ricotta salata over each serving with a vegetable peeler.

SERVES 6

Mezze Rigatoni with Oven-Roasted Zucchini and Pomodorini

This sauce is more about the zucchini, with a touch of sweet canned cherry tomatoes, called pomodorini, to make a sauce. Make this in the height of summer when zucchini are cheap and plentiful.

CALORIES PER SERVING:
442

2 pounds medium zucchini (5 or 6), cut into 1-inch cubes

3 tablespoons extra-virgin olive oil

Kosher salt

3 garlic cloves, sliced

1 cup chopped scallions

2 (14.5-ounce) cans peeled cherry tomatoes in juice

½ teaspoon dried oregano, preferably Sicilian oregano on the stalk

Crushed red pepper flakes

1 pound mezze rigatoni

1 cup fresh basil leaves, chopped

1 (2-ounce) piece ricotta salata

1. Preheat the oven to 450°F with a sheet pan on the middle rack.

2. Bring a large pot of salted water to a boil for pasta. In a large bowl, toss the zucchini with 1 tablespoon of the olive oil and season with salt. Spread on the preheated sheet pan and roast, tossing twice, until tender and browned all over, about 16 minutes.

3. Meanwhile, in a large skillet over medium-high heat, add the remaining 2 tablespoons olive oil. When the oil is hot, add the garlic and cook until fragrant, about 1 minute. Add the scallions and cook until wilted, about 3 minutes. Add the cherry tomatoes and oregano and season with salt and red pepper flakes. Bring to a simmer and add the roasted zucchini. Let simmer while you cook the pasta, breaking up the tomatoes a little with the back of a wooden spoon.

4. Add the mezze rigatoni to the boiling water. When the pasta is al dente, remove it with a spider or small strainer and add directly to the sauce, along with the basil, reserving the pasta water. Toss to coat the pasta in the sauce. Serve in warmed pasta bowls, shaving the ricotta salata over the pasta with a vegetable peeler.

SERVES 6

Cavatappi with Roasted Cherry Tomatoes, Garlic, and Ricotta Salata

These roasted cherry tomatoes are also good on their own, as a side to chicken or fish, or on a salad or sandwich. They will keep for several days in the refrigerator. The chopped pine nuts will help thicken the sauce as it cooks. Cavatappi are a fun pasta shape that spring up in the plate and have good curves for the sauce to hide in.

CALORIES PER SERVING:
446

3 tablespoons extra-virgin olive oil

5 garlic cloves, 2 finely chopped, 3 thinly sliced

1 teaspoon dried oregano, preferably Sicilian oregano on the stalk

6 cups halved grape or cherry tomatoes

Kosher salt

Crushed red pepper flakes

1 cup chopped scallions

¼ cup pine nuts, chopped

½ cup dry white wine

1 pound cavatappi

1 cup fresh basil leaves, chopped

⅓ cup freshly grated Grana Padano

1 (2-ounce) piece ricotta salata

1. Preheat the oven to 350°F.

2. Bring a large pot of salted water to a boil for pasta. In a large bowl, stir together 2 tablespoons of the olive oil, the chopped garlic, and the oregano. Add the tomatoes, season with salt and red pepper flakes, and toss to coat the tomatoes in the oil. Spread on a rimmed baking sheet and bake, stirring once or twice, until caramelized on the edges and shriveled but still pliable, 35 to 45 minutes (depending on the size of the tomatoes). Keep warm while you make the sauce.

3. In a large skillet over medium heat, add the remaining 1 tablespoon olive oil. When the oil is hot, add the sliced garlic and cook until golden on the edges and fragrant, about 1 minute. Add the scallions and cook until wilted, about 3 minutes. Add the pine nuts, let toast a minute, then increase the heat to medium-high and add the white wine. Cook until reduced by half, about 2 minutes, then ladle in 1 cup pasta water and simmer to reduce the sauce while you cook the pasta.

4. Add the cavatappi to the boiling water. When the pasta is al dente, remove it with a spider or small strainer and add directly to the sauce, reserving the pasta water. Add the basil and the roasted tomatoes and toss to coat the pasta with the sauce. Remove the skillet from the heat, add the grated Grana Padano, and toss. Shave the ricotta salata over the pasta with a vegetable peeler, toss gently, and serve.

SERVES 6

Fusilli with Tomatoes, Olives, and Capers (Puttanesca Style)

If you can find dried oregano from Sicily that is still on the stalk, buy it—it has a much less harsh flavor than bottled grocery store oregano. This is an aggressively seasoned dish, so go easy on the salt, but don't be afraid to have a heavy hand with the red pepper flakes.

CALORIES PER SERVING:
419

3 tablespoons extra-virgin olive oil

3 garlic cloves, thinly sliced

¾ cup pitted black Italian olives (such as Gaeta), coarsely chopped (about 20)

¼ cup capers in brine, drained

4 anchovy fillets

Kosher salt

Crushed red pepper flakes

1 (28-ounce) can whole San Marzano tomatoes, crushed by hand

½ teaspoon dried oregano, preferably Sicilian oregano on the stalk

1 pound fusilli

1 cup fresh Italian parsley leaves, chopped

½ cup freshly grated Grana Padano

1. Bring a large pot of salted water to a boil for pasta. In a large skillet over medium heat, add 2 tablespoons of the olive oil. When the oil is hot, add the garlic and let sizzle until golden on the edges, about 1 minute. Add the olives, capers, and anchovies. Cook and stir with a wooden spoon until the anchovies dissolve into the oil, about 2 minutes. Season with salt and red pepper flakes.

2. Add the tomatoes and 1 cup pasta water. Crumble in the dry oregano. Bring to a simmer and cook until thick and flavorful, about 20 minutes.

3. When the sauce is almost ready, add the fusilli to the boiling water. When the pasta is al dente, remove with a spider or small strainer and add directly to the sauce, reserving the pasta water. Add the parsley and the remaining 1 tablespoon olive oil. Toss to coat the pasta with the sauce, adding a splash of pasta water if the pasta seems dry. Remove the skillet from the heat, sprinkle with the grated Grana Padano, toss, and serve.

SERVES 6

Shells with Cherry Tomatoes and Sweet Peppers

Sweet mini bell peppers are widely available in grocery stores these days. They cook quickly and have a thin skin, so they don't need to be peeled and roasted to bring out their sweetness, like regular bell peppers. Once the cherry tomatoes go into the sauce, they also cook quickly, depending on their level of ripeness, so start cooking the pasta before you even add them.

CALORIES PER SERVING:
402

3 tablespoons extra-virgin olive oil

1 (8-ounce) package sweet mini bell peppers, seeded and sliced

2 cups chopped scallions

Kosher salt

Crushed red pepper flakes

6 sweet pickled cherry peppers, stemmed, seeded, and sliced, plus 2 tablespoons brine from the jar

2 cups halved cherry tomatoes

½ cup dry white wine

1 pound medium shells

1 cup fresh basil leaves, chopped

½ cup freshly grated Grana Padano

1. Bring a large pot of salted water to a boil for pasta. In a large skillet over medium heat, add the olive oil. When the oil is hot, add the bell peppers and cook, stirring often, until very tender, about 12 minutes.

2. Add the scallions and season with salt and red pepper flakes. Cook until the scallions are wilted, about 3 minutes. Increase the heat to medium-high and add the pickled cherry peppers. Once the cherry peppers are sizzling, add the cherry tomatoes and toss to coat in the oil. Add the white wine and pepper brine and cook until reduced by half, 3 to 4 minutes. Add ½ cup pasta water and bring to a simmer. Cook just until the tomatoes begin to fall apart and the sauce has reduced by about half, 2 to 3 minutes.

3. Meanwhile, add the shells to the boiling water. When the sauce is ready and the pasta is al dente, remove the pasta with a spider or small strainer and add directly to the sauce, reserving the pasta water. Add the basil and toss to coat the pasta with the sauce, adding a splash of pasta water if the pasta seems dry. Remove the skillet from the heat, sprinkle with the grated Grana Padano, toss, and serve.

SERVES 6

Spaghetti with Marinara Sauce

Most marinara sauces start with a lot of olive oil. As long as you've got good-quality ingredients—San Marzano tomatoes, fresh garlic and herbs—you don't need that much oil. Also, a lot of cooks make the mistake of overcooking their marinara sauce. Unlike a Bolognese or ragù, this should cook for 20 minutes maximum so the basic flavors stay bright. Spaghetti is a natural pairing with this pantry sauce, but almost any shape will do. This sauce freezes very well, so feel free to make a double batch and freeze half before you add the pasta and cheese.

CALORIES PER SERVING:
400

3 tablespoons extra-virgin olive oil

1 small onion, finely chopped (about ½ cup)

6 garlic cloves, thinly sliced

Kosher salt

Crushed red pepper flakes

1 (28-ounce) can whole San Marzano tomatoes, crushed by hand

1 pound spaghetti

2 cups fresh basil leaves. coarsely chopped

½ cup freshly grated Grana Padano

1. Bring a large pot of salted water to a boil for pasta. In a large skillet over medium heat, add the olive oil. When the oil is hot, add the onion. Toss to coat the onion in the oil and add a splash of pasta water. Cook until the onion is tender, about 6 minutes.

2. Increase the heat to medium-high to reduce away any excess pasta water, then add the garlic and cook until fragrant, about 1 minute. Season with salt and red pepper flakes. Add the tomatoes and 1 cup pasta water. Bring to a simmer and cook until slightly thickened, about 15 minutes.

3. Meanwhile, add the spaghetti to the boiling water. When the sauce is ready, stir in the basil. When the pasta is al dente, remove it with tongs and add directly to the sauce, reserving the pasta water. Toss to coat the pasta in the sauce, adding a splash of pasta water if the pasta seems dry. Remove the skillet from the heat, sprinkle with the grated Grana Padano, toss, and serve.

SERVES 6

Bucatini with Tomatoes and Prosciutto

For this sauce, have your deli person give you a couple of thick slices of prosciutto, then julienne them yourself. Pickled cherry peppers (hot or sweet) are another great, virtually no-calorie way to add a burst of flavor to many pasta recipes. If you're really a fan of heat, then buy the hot variety and leave the seeds in. Removing the seeds will provide moderate heat, while the sweet ones have no heat at all, just a pickly sweetness.

CALORIES PER SERVING:
411

2 tablespoons extra-virgin olive oil

2 ounces thickly sliced prosciutto, julienned

1 medium onion, sliced (about 1 cup)

5 hot pickled cherry peppers, stemmed, seeded (if desired), and thinly sliced, plus 1 tablespoon brine from the jar

1 (28-ounce) can whole San Marzano tomatoes, crushed by hand

Kosher salt

1 pound bucatini

1 cup fresh basil leaves, chopped

½ cup freshly grated Grana Padano

I. Bring a large pot of salted water to a boil for pasta. In a large skillet over medium heat, add the olive oil. When the oil is hot, add the prosciutto and cook until lightly browned, stirring occasionally, about 3 minutes. Add the onion and cook until softened, about 5 minutes.

2. Increase the heat to medium-high and add the cherry peppers. Once the cherry peppers begin to sizzle, add the brine, the tomatoes, and 1 cup pasta water. Bring to a simmer and season with salt. Simmer until slightly thickened and flavorful, about 15 minutes.

3. When the sauce is almost ready, add the bucatini to the boiling water. When the pasta is al dente, remove it with tongs and add directly to the sauce, reserving the pasta water. Add the basil and toss to coat the pasta with the sauce, adding a splash of pasta water if the pasta seems dry. Remove the skillet from the heat, sprinkle with the grated Grana Padano, toss, and serve.

SERVES 6

Gemelli with Peas and Prosciutto

In the spring, if you can get your hands on fresh peas, use them here—just cook them a few extra minutes. Fresh favas would also be a delicious addition or substitute for the peas.

CALORIES PER SERVING:
484

2 tablespoons extra-virgin olive oil

3 ounces thickly sliced prosciutto, julienned

2 medium leeks, white and light green parts, sliced (about 1 cup)

2 teaspoons fresh thyme leaves, chopped

½ cup dry white wine

2 cups canned whole San Marzano tomatoes, crushed by hand

¼ cup heavy cream

1½ cups frozen or fresh peas

1 pound gemelli

½ cup fresh basil leaves, chopped

½ cup freshly grated Grana Padano

1. Bring a large pot of salted water to a boil for pasta. In a large skillet over medium heat, add the olive oil. When the oil is hot, add the prosciutto and leeks and cook until the leeks are softened, about 7 minutes.

2. Add the thyme and cook until fragrant, about 1 minute. Increase the heat to medium-high and add the white wine. Simmer until reduced by half, about 2 minutes. Add the tomatoes and ¾ cup pasta water. Bring to a simmer and cook until slightly thickened, about 8 minutes. Add the cream and peas and simmer while you cook the pasta.

3. Add the gemelli to the boiling water. When the sauce is ready and the pasta is al dente, remove the pasta with a spider or small strainer and add directly to the sauce, reserving the pasta water. Add the basil and toss to coat the pasta in the sauce, adding a splash of pasta water if the pasta seems dry. Remove the skillet from the heat, sprinkle with the grated Grana Padano, toss, and serve.

SERVES 6

Bucatini with Mussels, Bacon, and Tomatoes

We remove the mussels from the shells for a more finished presentation, but you can leave them in for a casual family dinner. Don't overcook the mussels in the first stage, because they cook again a little in the sauce. Remove them from the heat just as they open.

CALORIES PER SERVING:
429

2 tablespoons extra-virgin olive oil

5 garlic cloves, thinly sliced

½ cup dry white wine

Kosher salt

Crushed red pepper flakes

2 pounds mussels, scrubbed and debearded

4 slices center-cut bacon, chopped

1 large onion, sliced (about 1½ cups)

1 (28-ounce) can whole San Marzano tomatoes, crushed by hand

2 fresh bay leaves

1 pound bucatini

1 cup fresh Italian parsley leaves, chopped

1. Bring a large pot of salted water to a boil for pasta. Heat a large Dutch oven over medium-high heat and add 1 tablespoon of the olive oil. When the oil is hot, add the garlic and let sizzle for a minute. Add the white wine and season with salt and red pepper flakes. Once the wine comes to a boil, add the mussels. Cover and simmer until the mussels open, about 4 minutes. Remove the mussels to a large bowl. Discard any mussels that didn't open. Strain and reserve the cooking juices. (You should have about 1 cup; if not, add pasta water to make 1 cup.) When the mussels are cooled, remove from the shells and discard the shells.

2. Heat a large skillet over medium heat. Add the remaining 1 tablespoon olive oil and the chopped bacon. Cook until the bacon renders its fat and begins to crisp, about 4 minutes. Add the onion and cook until tender, about 8 minutes. Add the tomatoes, cooking juices, and bay leaves. Season with salt and red pepper flakes. Simmer until the sauce has thickened, about 15 minutes.

3. When the sauce is almost ready, add the bucatini to the boiling water. When the pasta is al dente, remove it with tongs and add directly to the sauce, reserving the pasta water. Remove the bay leaves. Add the mussels and parsley. Toss until the mussels are heated through, adding a little pasta water if the pasta seems dry. Serve immediately.

SERVES 6

Orecchiette with Tomatoes, Prosciutto, and Cannellini Beans

If you have leftover cooked beans, you can use them here also. One can equals about 1½ cups cooked beans. We like to purchase organic canned beans because the beans are generally lower in sodium than most regular brands.

CALORIES PER SERVING:
460

2 tablespoons extra-virgin olive oil

2 ounces thickly sliced prosciutto, diced

1 medium onion, sliced (about 1 cup)

1 (15-ounce) can cannellini beans, rinsed and drained

3 garlic cloves, thinly sliced

2 teaspoons fresh rosemary needles, chopped

Kosher salt

Crushed red pepper flakes

1 (28-ounce) can whole San Marzano tomatoes, crushed by hand

2 fresh bay leaves

1 pound orecchiette

½ cup fresh Italian parsley leaves, chopped

½ cup freshly grated Grana Padano

1. Bring a large pot of salted water to a boil for pasta. In a large skillet over medium heat, add the olive oil. When the oil is hot, add the prosciutto. Cook until lightly browned, about 2 minutes, then add the onion. Cook until the onion is softened, about 5 minutes.

2. Add the cannellini beans and toss to coat in the oil. Add the garlic and rosemary and cook until fragrant, about 2 minutes. Season with salt and red pepper flakes. Add the tomatoes, bay leaves, and 1½ cups pasta water. Bring to a simmer and cook until thick and flavorful, about 20 minutes.

3. Meanwhile, add the orecchiette to the boiling water. When the sauce is ready and the pasta is al dente, remove the pasta with a spider or small strainer and add directly to the sauce, reserving the pasta water. Remove the bay leaves, add the parsley, and toss to coat the pasta in the sauce, adding a splash of pasta water if the pasta seems dry. Remove the skillet from the heat, sprinkle with the grated Grana Padano, toss, and serve.

SERVES 6

Ditalini with Lentils in Tomato Sauce

This dish works as either a soup course or a pasta course. Prepare it as written here for a thicker pasta dish or add up to 1½ cups more pasta water (½ cup at a time) at the end to thin the sauce to the consistency you like for soup. Lentils are also a starch, so less pasta is used in this recipe.

CALORIES PER SERVING:
410

1 large onion, cut into medium-size chunks

1 large carrot, cut into medium-size chunks

2 celery stalks, cut into medium-size chunks

3 ounces pancetta, cut into medium-size chunks

3 garlic cloves

2 tablespoons extra-virgin olive oil

3 tablespoons tomato paste

2 teaspoons fresh thyme leaves, chopped

Kosher salt

Crushed red pepper flakes

1½ cups brown lentils, rinsed well

1 fresh bay leaf

6 ounces ditalini

½ cup fresh Italian parsley leaves, chopped

½ cup freshly grated Grana Padano

1. In the work bowl of a food processor, combine the onion, carrot, celery, pancetta, and garlic. Pulse to make a smooth paste.

2. Heat a medium Dutch oven over medium-high heat and add the olive oil. When the oil is hot, scrape in the pancetta paste and cook, stirring occasionally, until the paste has dried out and just begins to stick to the bottom of the pot, about 7 minutes. Make a space in the pan, add the tomato paste, and let toast for a minute or two, then stir into the pancetta paste. Add the thyme and season with salt and red pepper flakes. Add the lentils and stir to coat them with the paste. Pour in 4 cups water, drop in the bay leaf, and bring to a simmer. Cook until the lentils are almost tender, 25 to 30 minutes.

3. Once the lentils are almost done, stir in 2 cups water, the ditalini, and parsley. Cook until the ditalini are al dente, 8 to 10 minutes, adding a little more water at the end if the pasta absorbs too much. Remove the bay leaf. Ladle into warm soup bowls, sprinkle with some of the grated Grana Padano, and serve.

SERVES 6

Spaghetti Fra Diavolo with Shrimp

Crushed red pepper flakes and hot pickled cherry peppers add two kinds of heat to this spicy shrimp dish. For even more heat, leave the seeds in the peppers.

CALORIES PER SERVING:
445

2 tablespoons extra-virgin olive oil

1 pound large shrimp, peeled and deveined

Kosher salt

4 garlic cloves, sliced

4 hot pickled cherry peppers, stemmed, seeded (if desired), and sliced, plus 2 tablespoons brine from the jar

2 anchovy fillets

½ teaspoon crushed red pepper flakes, plus more for garnish

½ cup dry white wine

1 (28-ounce) can whole San Marzano tomatoes, crushed by hand

½ teaspoon dried oregano, preferably Sicilian oregano on the stalk

1 pound spaghetti

½ cup fresh basil leaves, chopped

½ cup fresh Italian parsley leaves, chopped

1. Bring a large pot of salted water to a boil for pasta. In a large nonstick skillet over medium-high heat, add 1 tablespoon of the olive oil. When the oil is hot, add the shrimp and season with salt. Cook just until browned on both sides, 1 to 2 minutes per side. Remove to a plate while you make the sauce.

2. Add the remaining 1 tablespoon olive oil to the skillet. When the oil is hot, add the garlic, cherry peppers, anchovies, and red pepper flakes. Cook until sizzling and fragrant, about 2 minutes. Add the white wine and brine from the peppers. Bring to a simmer and reduce by half, 2 to 3 minutes. Add the tomatoes and 1 cup pasta water. Bring to a simmer, add the oregano, and season with salt. Simmer until the sauce has thickened, about 15 minutes.

3. Meanwhile, add the spaghetti to the boiling water. When the sauce is thickened, add the shrimp and any cooking juices from the plate. Simmer until the shrimp are just cooked through, 2 to 3 minutes. Add the basil and parsley. When the pasta is al dente, remove it with tongs and add directly to the sauce, reserving the pasta water. Toss to coat the pasta with the sauce, adding a splash of pasta water if the pasta seems dry. Serve immediately, sprinkling with more red pepper flakes, if desired.

SERVES 6

Linguine in Saffron Tomato Sauce with Calamari

Choose smaller, tender calamari, less than 4 or 5 inches long. Don't overcook them or they'll be chewy—all they need is a quick dip in the tomato sauce. Take time to sweat the vegetables, as they form the basis for this dish. The saffron adds another level and is a natural pairing with seafood. You could substitute shrimp, clams, mussels, or scallops (or a combination) for the calamari; just alter the cooking time accordingly.

CALORIES PER SERVING:
439

2 tablespoons extra-virgin olive oil

1 medium carrot, finely diced (about 1 cup)

2 stalks celery, finely diced (about 1 cup)

a small bulb fennel, cored and thinly sliced (about 2 cups), plus ¼ cup tender fronds, chopped

1 cup chopped scallions

4 cloves garlic, sliced

Kosher salt

Crushed red pepper flakes

Large pinch of saffron

½ cup dry white wine

1 (28-ounce) can whole San Marzano tomatoes, crushed by hand

1 pound linguine

12 ounces medium to small calamari, cleaned, tubes cut in ½-inch rings, tentacles halved lengthwise

1 cup fresh Italian parsley leaves, chopped

I. Bring a large pot of salted water to a boil for pasta. In a large skillet over medium-low heat, add the olive oil. When the oil is hot, add the carrot, celery, fennel (reserving the fronds), and a big splash of pasta water. Cook, stirring often, until vegetables are tender, about 10 minutes.

2. Increase heat to medium-high and boil away any excess liquid in the skillet. Add the scallions and cook until wilted, about 3 minutes. Add the garlic and cook until fragrant, about 1 minute. Season with salt and red pepper flakes. Add the saffron and white wine, and boil until reduced by about half. Add the tomatoes and 1 cup pasta water. Bring to a simmer and cook until thickened, about 10 minutes.

3. Meanwhile, add the linguine to the boiling water. When the sauce has thickened, add the calamari and chopped parsley to it and toss to coat the calamari in the sauce. Let cook just until calamari turns white, 2 to 3 minutes. When the linguine is al dente, transfer with tongs directly to the sauce, reserving the pasta water. Working quickly, so that the calamari doesn't overcook, toss to coat the pasta with the sauce, adding a splash of pasta water if the pasta seems dry. Garnish with the reserved fennel fronds and serve immediately.

SERVES 6

Linguine with Tomatoes, Capers, and Tuna

Cheese doesn't really work with this sauce, but we've added a little garnish of toasted bread crumbs for texture. You could also use toasted panko if you don't have time to make your own crumbs. Water-packed white tuna has about half the calories as oil-packed light tuna, so it's a smart choice here.

CALORIES PER SERVING:
435

3 tablespoons extra-virgin olive oil

1 (2-ounce) piece stale country bread, grated on the coarse holes of a box grater (1¼ cups crumbs)

½ cup fresh Italian parsley leaves, chopped

Kosher salt

6 garlic cloves, thinly sliced

¼ cup capers in brine, drained

3 anchovy fillets

Crushed red pepper flakes

1 (28-ounce) can whole San Marzano tomatoes, crushed by hand

2 (5-ounce) cans water-packed white tuna, drained

1 pound linguine

1. Bring a large pot of salted water to a boil for pasta. In a small skillet, heat 1 tablespoon of the olive oil over medium heat. Add the bread crumbs. Toss and cook until the crumbs are crisp and golden, 5 to 6 minutes. Scrape into a small bowl. Stir in half of the parsley and season with salt.

2. In a large skillet over medium heat, add the remaining 2 tablespoons olive oil. When the oil is hot, add the garlic and cook until fragrant and golden on the edges, 1 to 2 minutes, taking care not to burn it. Increase the heat to medium-high and add the capers and anchovies. Cook and stir to dissolve the anchovies into the oil. Season with red pepper flakes. Add the tomatoes and 1 cup pasta water. Bring the sauce to a simmer and simmer for 5 minutes to blend the flavors. Add the tuna, stir to combine, but don't break up the tuna too much. Season with salt and simmer gently until thickened, about 10 minutes more.

3. Meanwhile, add the linguine to the boiling water. When the pasta is al dente, remove it with tongs and add directly to the sauce, reserving the pasta water. Add the remaining parsley and toss to coat the pasta with the sauce, adding a splash of pasta water if the pasta seems dry. Serve in warmed pasta bowls, sprinkled with the bread crumbs.

SERVES 6

Carne

Meats

Rigatoni with Chicken and Zucchini

Chicken thighs do have a little more fat than chicken breasts, but they are really the right choice for a long, slow braise. Just three-quarters of a pound will add a deep, rich flavor to this sauce.

CALORIES PER SERVING:
475

2 tablespoons extra-virgin olive oil

12 ounces boneless, skinless chicken thighs, trimmed of excess fat and diced into ½-inch cubes

2 leeks, white and light green parts, sliced (about 1 cup)

3 medium zucchini cut into ½-inch dice (about 4 cups)

Kosher salt

Crushed red pepper flakes

3 garlic cloves, thinly sliced

8 fresh sage leaves, chopped

1 (28-ounce) can whole San Marzano tomatoes, crushed by hand

2 fresh bay leaves

1 pound rigatoni

½ cup fresh Italian parsley leaves, chopped

½ cup freshly grated Grana Padano

1. Bring a large pot of salted water to a boil for pasta. Heat a large skillet over medium-high heat. Add 1 tablespoon of the olive oil. When the oil is hot, add the chicken thighs and cook, tossing occasionally, until browned all over, about 4 minutes. Remove to a plate.

2. Add the remaining 1 tablespoon olive oil to the skillet. When the oil is hot, add the leeks and sauté until tender, about 4 minutes. Add the zucchini and season with salt and red pepper flakes. Toss and cook until the zucchini is browned on the edges, about 4 minutes. Add the garlic and sage and cook until fragrant, about 1 minute. Add the tomatoes, bay leaves, and 1 cup pasta water. Bring to a simmer and add the chicken back to the sauce. Simmer until the chicken is very tender, about 20 minutes.

3. When the sauce is almost ready, add the rigatoni to the boiling water. When the pasta is al dente, remove it with a spider or small strainer and add directly to the sauce, along with the parsley, reserving the pasta water. Toss to coat the pasta with the sauce, adding a splash of pasta water if the pasta seems dry. Remove and discard the bay leaves. Remove the skillet from the heat, sprinkle with the grated Grana Padano, toss, and serve.

SERVES 6

Rotini with Chicken, Onions, and Porcini

A variation on the recipe could be to double the chicken thighs and skip shredding them at the end. That makes a great stew, although it also raises the calorie count.

CALORIES PER SERVING: 492

½ ounce dried porcini mushrooms (about 1 cup loosely packed)

1½ tablespoons extra-virgin olive oil

12 ounces boneless, skinless chicken thighs, trimmed of excess fat

2 ounces pancetta, diced

2 large onions, sliced (about 3 cups)

1 tablespoon fresh thyme leaves, chopped

¾ cup dry red wine

2 cups low-sodium chicken broth

2 fresh bay leaves

1 (2-inch) piece Grana Padano rind

1 pound rotini

½ cup fresh Italian parsley leaves, chopped

½ cup freshly grated Grana Padano

1. Bring a large pot of salted water to a boil for pasta. Ladle 1 cup hot pasta water into a spouted measuring cup and add the porcini. Let soak until softened, about 15 minutes. Drain and chop the mushrooms. Strain and reserve the soaking water.

2. In a large Dutch oven over medium heat, heat the olive oil. Brown the chicken thighs on all sides, about 2 minutes per side, and remove to a plate. Add the pancetta to the pot and cook until the fat is rendered, about 4 minutes. Add the onions and cook until golden, about 15 minutes.

3. Add the thyme and cook until fragrant, about 1 minute. Add the red wine, bring to a boil, and cook until reduced by half, about 2 minutes. Add the chopped porcini, the soaking liquid, and chicken broth. Bring to a simmer and add the chicken thighs, bay leaves, and cheese rind. Cover and cook until the chicken is very tender, about 20 minutes. Remove the chicken, let cool slightly, then shred (or chop) and add back into the sauce. While the chicken is cooling, increase the heat under the sauce and boil to thicken the sauce. Remove and discard the cheese rind and bay leaves.

4. Add the rotini to the boiling water. When the pasta is al dente, remove it with a spider or small strainer and add directly to the sauce, along with the parsley, reserving the pasta water. Toss to coat the pasta with the sauce, adding a splash of pasta water if the pasta seems dry. Remove the pot from the heat, sprinkle with the grated Grana Padano, toss, and serve.

SERVES 6

Spaghetti with Turkey Meatballs

The vegetable paste here does double duty—adding moisture and flavor to the meatballs (without a lot of calories) and creating a base for the tomato sauce. Baking the meatballs at a high temperature is like browning them, but without as much oil. If the sauce seems watery, any extra liquid will cook down and soak into the meatballs as they simmer.

CALORIES PER SERVING:
496

1 medium onion, cut into medium-size chunks

1 small carrot, cut into medium-size chunks

1 celery stalk, cut into medium-size chunks

½ cup fresh Italian parsley

3 garlic cloves, crushed and peeled

1 pound ground turkey breast

1 large egg, beaten

½ cup freshly grated Grana Padano

⅓ cup unseasoned dried bread crumbs

Kosher salt

2 tablespoons extra-virgin olive oil

1 (28-ounce) can whole San Marzano tomatoes, crushed by hand

1 teaspoon dried oregano, preferably Sicilian oregano

Crushed red pepper flakes

1 pound spaghetti

½ cup fresh basil leaves, chopped

1. Preheat the oven to 450°F.

2. In the work bowl of a food processor, combine the onion, carrot, celery, parsley, and garlic and process to make a smooth paste. Scrape half of the vegetable paste into a large bowl and set the rest aside in a small bowl.

3. Line a sheet pan with parchment paper. To the large bowl, add the turkey, egg, ¼ cup of the grated Grana Padano, and the bread crumbs. Season with 1 teaspoon salt. Mix with your hands until just combined. (If you like, you can fry a small patty to taste for seasoning.) Form into 18 meatballs and put on the lined sheet pan. Bake until the meatballs are firm (but they don't have to be cooked through), about 12 minutes.

4. Meanwhile, bring a large pot of salted water to a boil for pasta. In a medium Dutch oven over medium-high heat, heat the olive oil. When the oil is hot, add the remaining vegetable paste and cook, stirring, until it dries out and begins to stick to the bottom of the pan (turn the heat down if it begins to burn toward the end). Add the tomatoes and 3 cups pasta water. Bring to a simmer and add the oregano. Season with salt and red pepper flakes. Add the meatballs to the sauce. Simmer until the meatballs are cooked through and the sauce is thick and flavorful, about 30 minutes.

5. Add the spaghetti to the boiling water. When the pasta is almost al dente, remove the meatballs from the sauce to a warm bowl and add the basil to the sauce. When the pasta is al dente, remove it with tongs and add directly to the sauce, reserving the pasta water. Toss to coat the pasta with the sauce, adding a splash of pasta water if the pasta seems dry. Remove the pot from the heat, sprinkle with the remaining grated Grano Padano, and serve in warm pasta bowls, with meatballs on top.

SERVES 6

Ziti with Turkey Piccata and Spinach

You can use turkey cutlets or tenders for this dish. You can also cut thin paillards from a boneless, skinless turkey breast; they should be about ½ inch thick. Turkey is slightly lower in protein than chicken, but it has 75 percent less fat. So you can substitute chicken, but it will be higher in calories.

CALORIES PER SERVING:
431

12 ounces turkey breast cutlets, cut against the grain into ½-inch strips

Kosher salt

Crushed red pepper flakes

2 tablespoons all-purpose flour

1 tablespoon extra-virgin olive oil

2 tablespoons unsalted butter

2 large shallots, chopped (about ½ cup)

¼ cup capers in brine, drained

Juice of 1 lemon

½ cup dry white wine

1½ cups low-sodium chicken broth

1 pound ziti

1 (6-ounce) bag baby spinach

1 cup fresh Italian parsley leaves, chopped

½ cup freshly grated Grana Padano

1. Bring a large pot of salted water to a boil for pasta. Season the turkey with salt and red pepper flakes. In a large bowl, toss the turkey with the flour, discarding any excess flour.

2. Heat a large nonstick skillet over medium-high heat. Add the olive oil. When the oil is hot, add the turkey strips in one layer and brown on both sides, 3 to 4 minutes in all. Remove to a plate.

3. Reduce the heat to medium and add the butter. When the butter is melted, add the shallots and cook until softened, about 6 minutes. Add the capers and let them sizzle a minute, then add the lemon juice and white wine. Bring to a boil and cook until reduced by half, about 2 minutes. Add the chicken broth and bring to a simmer.

4. Once the sauce is simmering, add the ziti to the boiling water. After the pasta has been boiling for about 5 minutes, add the spinach and turkey to the sauce. When the pasta is al dente, remove it with a spider or small strainer and add directly to the sauce, reserving the pasta water. Add the parsley and toss to coat the pasta with the sauce, adding a splash of pasta water if the pasta seems dry. Remove the skillet from the heat, sprinkle with the grated Grana Padano, toss, and serve.

SERVES 6

Fettuccine with Chicken Livers, Bacon, and Sage

Chicken livers have a strong taste, so a small amount brings a deep, rich flavor to this dish. Trim and rinse the livers well and pat very dry so that they don't splatter when you sauté them. For those eating gluten-free, they can use gluten-free pasta in any recipe in the book, as a one-to-one swap. Calories may vary slightly depending on the brand, but not much.

CALORIES PER SERVING: 423

1 tablespoon extra-virgin olive oil

3 slices center-cut bacon, chopped

1 large onion, sliced (about 1½ cups)

8 ounces chicken livers, trimmed, chopped into ½-inch pieces, and patted dry

Kosher salt

Crushed red pepper flakes

10 fresh sage leaves, chopped

1 tablespoon sherry vinegar

¾ cup dry white wine

1 pound fettuccine

3½ cups loosely packed baby spinach (about 4 to 5 ounces)

½ cup fresh Italian parsley leaves, chopped

½ cup freshly grated Grana Padano

I. Bring a large pot of salted water to a boil for pasta. Heat a large skillet over medium heat. When the skillet is hot, add the olive oil. Add the bacon and cook until the fat is rendered, about 3 minutes. Add the onion and cook, stirring occasionally, until the onion is soft and golden, about 15 minutes.

2. Increase the heat to medium-high and add the chicken livers. Cook until browned all over, about 3 minutes. Season with salt and red pepper flakes. Add the sage and cook until fragrant, about 1 minute. Add the vinegar and cook until it reduces away and glazes the onions, about 1 minute. Add the white wine and reduce by half, about 2 minutes. Add 1 cup pasta water and simmer until the chicken livers are tender, about 5 minutes.

3. Add the fettuccine to the boiling water. Once the pasta is cooking, add the spinach to the sauce. When the pasta is al dente, remove it with tongs and add directly to the sauce, reserving the pasta water. Add the parsley and toss to coat the pasta with the sauce, adding a splash of pasta water if the pasta seems dry. Remove the skillet from the heat, sprinkle with the grated Grana Padano, toss, and serve.

SERVES 6

Cavatappi with Veal Spezzatino

Veal spezzatino is traditionally just veal stew, but this one uses less meat and more vegetables, turning it into a perfect pasta sauce. The long cooking time adds a velvety richness to the sauce and creates veal chunks that break apart and melt in your mouth.

CALORIES PER SERVING:
474

12 ounces boneless veal stew meat (from the shoulder, trimmed of fat), cut into 1-inch cubes

Kosher salt

2 tablespoons extra-virgin olive oil

1 pound mixed mushrooms, thickly sliced (about 8 cups)

1 large onion, chopped

1 large carrot, chopped

2 celery stalks, chopped

2 garlic cloves, thinly sliced

1 tablespoon fresh thyme leaves, chopped

1 tablespoon fresh sage leaves, chopped

3 tablespoons tomato paste

½ cup dry red wine

4 cups low-sodium chicken broth

2 fresh bay leaves

Crushed red pepper flakes

1 pound cavatappi

½ cup fresh Italian parsley leaves, chopped

½ cup freshly grated Grana Padano

1. Pat the veal dry and season with salt. Heat a large Dutch oven over medium-high heat. Add the oil. When the oil is hot, add the veal and brown all over, about 5 minutes. Remove to a plate. Add the mushrooms and cook, without stirring, until browned on the underside, then stir and brown again, about 5 minutes in all.

2. Reduce the heat to medium and add the onion, carrot, and celery. Cook, stirring often, until the vegetables have begun to soften, about 6 minutes. Add the garlic, thyme, and sage and cook until fragrant, about 1 minute. Make a space in the pan and add the tomato paste. Cook, stirring in that spot, until the tomato paste toasts and darkens a shade or two, 1 to 2 minutes. Stir the tomato paste into the vegetables and add the red wine. Bring to a simmer, then add the chicken broth and bring to a simmer again. Add the bay leaves and season with salt and red pepper flakes. Add back the veal, bring to a simmer, cover, and cook until the veal is very tender, about 1 hour. Uncover and increase the heat to reduce the sauce by about half, 2 to 3 minutes (depending on how thick you like your sauce), pressing on the veal with a wooden spoon to shred it a little bit.

3. Meanwhile, bring a large pot of salted water to a boil. Add the cavatappi to the boiling water. When the pasta is al dente, remove it with a spider or small strainer and add directly to the sauce, along with the parsley, reserving the pasta water. Toss to coat the pasta with the sauce, adding a splash of pasta water if the pasta seems dry. Remove the bay leaves. Remove the pot from the heat, sprinkle with the grated Grana Padano, toss, and serve.

SERVES 6

Ziti with Tomato and Chicken Liver Sauce

Leeks and peas add a touch of springtime to this hearty pasta sauce. When working with chicken livers, make sure you trim away any fat and sinew, leaving just the liver.

CALORIES PER SERVING:
454

2 tablespoons extra-virgin olive oil

2 medium leeks, white and light green parts, sliced (about 1 cup)

8 ounces chicken livers, trimmed, patted dry, and chopped

Kosher salt

Crushed red pepper flakes

3 garlic cloves, thinly sliced

2 teaspoons fresh rosemary needles, chopped

½ cup dry white wine

1 (28-ounce) can whole San Marzano tomatoes, crushed by hand

1 pound ziti

1 cup frozen peas

1 cup fresh Italian parsley leaves, chopped

½ cup freshly grated Grana Padano

I. Bring a large pot of salted water to a boil for pasta. Heat a large skillet over medium heat. Add the olive oil. When the oil is hot, add the leeks and cook until softened, about 5 minutes. Add the chicken livers and cook until no longer pink, about 3 minutes. Season with salt and red pepper flakes and add the garlic and rosemary. Cook until fragrant, about 1 minute. Add the white wine and cook until reduced by half, about 2 minutes. Add the tomatoes and 1 cup pasta water. Bring to a simmer and cook until the chicken livers are very tender, about 10 minutes.

2. Add the ziti to the boiling water. Once the pasta is cooking, add the peas and parsley to the simmering sauce. When the pasta is al dente, remove it with a spider or small strainer and add directly to the sauce, reserving the pasta water. Toss to coat the pasta with the sauce, adding a splash of pasta water if the pasta seems dry. Remove the skillet from the heat, sprinkle with the grated Grana Padano, toss, and serve.

SERVES 6

Spaghetti Bolognese

If you're so inclined, make a double batch and save the rest, because this sauce freezes very well. We added more vegetables and less meat and chose leaner meats to save calories. As a tip, if you have a meat grinder or food processor, you can buy the lean cuts and grind them yourself.

CALORIES PER SERVING:
500

2 cups low-sodium chicken broth

1 tablespoon extra-virgin olive oil

2 ounces pancetta, finely chopped

1 cup finely chopped onions

¾ cup finely chopped carrots

¾ cup finely chopped celery

3 garlic cloves, chopped

8 ounces 95% lean ground beef

4 ounces lean ground pork

4 ounces ground veal

¼ cup dry red wine

2 cups whole canned San Marzano tomatoes, crushed by hand

Kosher salt

Crushed red pepper flakes

2 fresh bay leaves

1 pound spaghetti

½ cup freshly grated Grana Padano

1. In a small saucepan, bring the chicken broth and 2 cups water just to a simmer. Heat a large Dutch oven over medium heat. Add the olive oil. When the oil is hot, add the pancetta and cook until the fat is rendered, about 4 minutes. Add the onions, carrots, and celery and cook until almost tender, about 8 minutes. Add the garlic and cook until fragrant, about 1 minute. Add the ground beef, pork, and veal and break up with a wooden spoon. Cook until the meats release their juices, then increase the heat to medium-high to reduce the liquid and brown the meat, about 15 minutes in all.

2. Pour in the red wine and cook until reduced, about 2 minutes. Add the tomatoes and enough of the simmering broth to just cover the meat. Season with salt and red pepper flakes and add the bay leaves. Partially cover the pot and simmer, adding the broth as needed to keep the meat covered, until the vegetables are very tender and the sauce is thick and flavorful, about 1½ hours. (You should use up all of the broth by the end of the cooking time.) Remove the bay leaves.

3. Bring a large pot of salted water to a boil for pasta. Add the spaghetti to the boiling water. When the pasta is al dente, remove it with tongs and add directly to the sauce, reserving the pasta water. Toss to coat the pasta with the sauce, adding a splash of pasta water if the pasta seems dry. Remove the pot from the heat, sprinkle with the grated Grana Padano, toss, and serve.

SERVES 6

Bucatini with Sausage and Peppers

This recipe is a prime example of how to cut calories without sacrificing flavor. We use a ton of vegetables and just a handful of flavorful sausage. Don't skimp on the time needed to wilt down the vegetables, because that time adds sweetness to the sauce.

CALORIES PER SERVING:
400

1 tablespoon extra-virgin olive oil

8 ounces sweet Italian turkey sausage (2 links), removed from casings

1 large onion, sliced (about 1½ cups)

1 medium red bell pepper, sliced (about 1½ cups)

1 medium yellow bell pepper, sliced (about 1½ cups)

4 garlic cloves, thinly sliced

¼ cup dry white wine

1 (28-ounce) can whole San Marzano tomatoes, crushed by hand

1 teaspoon dried oregano, preferably Sicilian oregano on the stalk

Kosher salt

Crushed red pepper flakes

1 pound bucatini

½ cup fresh Italian parsley leaves, chopped

½ cup freshly grated Grana Padano

1. Bring a large pot of salted water to a boil for pasta. In a large skillet over medium-high heat, add the olive oil. Add the sausage. Cook and crumble with a wooden spoon until the sausage is well browned, about 4 minutes. Reduce the heat to medium, add the onion, red bell pepper, and yellow bell pepper and cook until wilted, about 8 minutes, adding a splash of pasta water if the pan seems dry at any point.

2. Add the garlic and cook until fragrant, about 1 minute. Pour in the wine and reduce, about 2 minutes. Add the tomatoes and 2 cups pasta water. Stir in the oregano and season with salt and red pepper flakes. Adjust the heat to maintain a simmer and cook until thick and flavorful, about 20 minutes.

3. When the sauce is almost ready, add the bucatini to the boiling water. When the pasta is al dente, remove it with tongs and add directly to the sauce, reserving the pasta water. Add the parsley. Toss to coat the pasta in the sauce, adding a splash of pasta water if the pasta seems dry. Remove the skillet from the heat, sprinkle with the grated Grana Padano, toss, and serve.

SERVES 6

Mezze Rigatoni with Fennel and Sausage

This dish gets its intense fennel taste from three sources—the sausage, the fresh fennel, and a little ground fennel. For the most flavor, toast dry fennel seeds and grind them to a powder yourself (in a spice grinder) just before you're ready to use them. Store-bought powder is dried out and delivers less flavor.

CALORIES PER SERVING: 466

1 tablespoon extra-virgin olive oil

12 ounces sweet Italian turkey sausage with fennel seeds (3 or 4 links), removed from casings

2 small fennel bulbs, cored and thinly sliced (about 3 cups), plus 1 cup fronds, chopped

1 large onion, sliced (about 1½ cups)

Kosher salt

Crushed red pepper flakes

3 garlic cloves, thinly sliced

½ teaspoon ground fennel seeds

3 tablespoons tomato paste

½ cup dry white wine

1 pound mezze rigatoni

½ cup fresh Italian parsley leaves, chopped

½ cup freshly grated Grana Padano

I. Bring a large pot of salted water to a boil for pasta. In a large skillet over medium heat, add the olive oil. When the oil is hot, add the sausage. Cook and crumble with a wooden spoon until the sausage is lightly browned, about 4 minutes. Add the sliced fennel and onion and cook until softened and golden, about 20 minutes. (Adjust the heat or add a splash of pasta water if it seems as if the onion and fennel are getting too dark too quickly.) Season with salt and red pepper flakes.

2. Increase the heat to medium-high and add the garlic and ground fennel. Cook until fragrant, about 1 minute. Make a space in the pan and add the tomato paste. Cook, stirring in that spot, until the tomato paste toasts and darkens a shade or two, about 2 minutes. Stir the tomato paste into the vegetables. Add the white wine and bring to a rapid simmer. Add 1½ cups pasta water and simmer until the vegetables are very tender, about 10 minutes.

3. Meanwhile, add the mezze rigatoni to the boiling water. When the sauce is ready and the pasta is al dente, remove the pasta with a spider or small strainer and add directly to the sauce, reserving the pasta water. Add the reserved fennel fronds and the parsley and toss to coat the pasta with the sauce, adding a splash of pasta water if the pasta seems dry. Remove the skillet from the heat, sprinkle with the grated Grana Padano, toss, and serve.

SERVES 6

Bucatini with a Quick Meat Sauce

Bolognese is a long-cooking sauce, usually reserved for a weekend or a special meal. This is a light but flavorful meat sauce made in less than half the time.

CALORIES PER SERVING:
486

2 tablespoons extra-virgin olive oil

12 ounces 90% lean ground sirloin

1 small onion, finely chopped (about ¾ cup)

1 small carrot, finely chopped (about ½ cup)

2 small celery stalks, finely chopped (about ½ cup)

2 garlic cloves, chopped

Kosher salt

Crushed red pepper flakes

1 (28-ounce) can whole San Marzano tomatoes, crushed by hand

1 teaspoon dried oregano, preferably Sicilian oregano on the stalk

1 pound bucatini

½ cup fresh basil leaves, chopped

½ cup fresh Italian parsley leaves, chopped

½ cup freshly grated Grana Padano

I. Bring a large pot of salted water to a boil for pasta. In a large skillet over medium heat, add the olive oil. When the oil is hot, add the ground sirloin and cook until browned, about 4 minutes. Add the onion, carrot, and celery and cook until the onion is softened, about 6 minutes. Add the garlic and cook until fragrant, about 1 minute. Season with salt and red pepper flakes. Add the tomatoes and rinse out the can with 1 cup pasta water. Sprinkle in the oregano and simmer the sauce until thick and flavorful, about 20 minutes.

2. When the sauce is about halfway done, add the bucatini to the boiling water. When the pasta is al dente, remove it with tongs and add directly to the sauce, along with the basil and parsley, reserving the pasta water. Toss to coat the pasta with the sauce, adding a splash of pasta water if the pasta seems dry. Remove the skillet from the heat, sprinkle with the grated Grana Padano, toss, and serve.

SERVES 6

Ziti with Smoked Pork and Cabbage

The smoked pork chops are already cooked, so they don't need a lot of time to add a deep smoky flavor to the sauce. Add them back once the cabbage begins to soften to keep them from drying out. Most good butcher shops and some large grocery stores carry precut smoked pork chops. If you can find them only on the bone, just trim the meat from the bone for this recipe and save that bone to flavor a soup!

CALORIES PER SERVING:
462

2 tablespoons extra-virgin olive oil

12 ounces boneless smoked pork chops

1 large onion, sliced (about 1½ cups)

1 small head savoy cabbage, coarsely shredded (about 10 cups)

1 tablespoon fresh thyme leaves, chopped

1 tablespoon fresh sage leaves, chopped

Kosher salt

Crushed red pepper flakes

2 tablespoons tomato paste

1 teaspoon smoked paprika

½ cup dry white wine

1 pound ziti

½ cup freshly grated Grana Padano

1. Bring a large pot of salted water to a boil for pasta. In a large Dutch oven over medium heat, add the olive oil. When the oil is hot, brown the pork chops on both sides and remove to a plate. Once cooled, cut the pork chops into small chunks.

2. To the Dutch oven, add the onion and cook until just softened, about 8 minutes. Add the cabbage, thyme, and sage and season with salt and red pepper flakes. Cook, stirring often, until the cabbage begins to wilt, about 5 minutes. Make a space in the pan and add the tomato paste. Cook, stirring in that spot, until the tomato paste toasts and is a shade or two darker, about 2 minutes. Stir the tomato paste into the vegetables. Add the paprika and white wine and bring to a simmer. Add 1½ cups pasta water. Simmer, covered, until the cabbage has totally wilted, about 20 minutes. Add the chopped pork (and another ½ cup pasta water if the water has evaporated away) and simmer until the cabbage is very tender and the sauce is thick and flavorful, about 15 minutes.

3. Add the ziti to the boiling water. When the pasta is al dente, remove it with a spider or small strainer and add directly to the sauce, reserving the pasta water. Toss to coat the pasta with the sauce, adding a splash of pasta water if the pasta seems dry. Remove the pot from the heat, sprinkle with the grated Grana Padano, toss, and serve.

SERVES 6

Linguine with Sausage, Greens, and Egg Pan Sauce

Think of this as a riff on carbonara, but slightly less rich, with the addition of some hearty greens. When making this dish, have all of your ingredients prepped and ready to go and serve as soon as it is finished—the eggs don't hold well.

CALORIES PER SERVING:
468

2 tablespoons extra-virgin olive oil

8 ounces sweet Italian turkey sausage (2 links), removed from casings

1 cup chopped scallions

3 garlic cloves, thinly sliced

1 small head escarole, coarsely chopped (about 6 cups)

1 small head kale, coarsely chopped (about 4 cups)

Kosher salt

Crushed red pepper flakes

1 pound linguine

3 large eggs

¼ cup nonfat milk

½ cup freshly grated Grana Padano

1. Bring a large pot of salted water to a boil for pasta. In a large skillet over medium heat, add the olive oil. When the oil is hot, add the sausage. Cook and crumble with a wooden spoon until no longer pink, about 4 minutes. Add the scallions and cook until wilted, about 3 minutes. Add the garlic and let sizzle a minute, then add the escarole and kale. Season with salt and red pepper flakes and toss to coat in the oil. Cook until the greens are wilted, about 5 minutes, then add ½ cup pasta water. Cover and simmer until the greens are tender, about 8 minutes.

2. Meanwhile, add the linguine to the boiling water. In a medium bowl, whisk the eggs with the milk and a pinch of salt. When the greens are tender and the pasta is al dente, remove the pasta with tongs and add directly to the greens. Whisk ¼ cup hot pasta water into the egg mixture to temper it, then pour the eggs over the pasta, tossing constantly to coat the pasta in a loose scramble of eggs, about 1 minute. Remove the skillet from the heat, sprinkle with the grated Grana Padano, toss, and serve immediately.

SERVES 6

Rigatoni with Lamb and Eggplant

Ground lamb has a lot of flavor, so a little goes a long way. You can also make this recipe with lean ground sirloin. This is good to prepare ahead, so consider making a double batch and freezing the rest. Choose firm, heavy, shiny eggplants—smaller Italian eggplants have fewer seeds and are less bitter so you can usually skip salting them, but for large, seedy ones, salt the cubes, drain in a colander for 30 minutes, rinse, dry, and proceed. Pecorino Romano is a natural fit with lamb, but you can use Grana Padano if you prefer.

CALORIES PER SERVING:
491

1½ tablespoons extra-virgin olive oil

3 small Italian eggplants, cut into 1-inch cubes (about 5 cups)

Kosher salt

8 ounces lean ground lamb

1 medium onion, chopped (about 1 cup)

1 medium carrot, chopped (about ¾ cup)

1 tablespoon fresh thyme leaves, chopped

½ teaspoon smoked paprika

¼ teaspoon ground cinnamon

1 (28-ounce) can whole San Marzano tomatoes, crushed by hand

2 fresh bay leaves

Crushed red pepper flakes

1 pound rigatoni

½ cup fresh Italian parsley leaves, chopped

½ cup freshly grated Pecorino Romano

1. Bring a large pot of salted water to a boil for pasta. In a large skillet over medium heat, add 1 tablespoon of the olive oil. When the oil is hot, add the eggplants and season with salt. Cook and stir until the eggplant has browned all over, about 6 minutes, then remove to a plate.

2. Add the remaining ½ tablespoon olive oil. When the oil is hot, add the lamb and brown all over, about 4 minutes. Add the onion and carrot and cook until the onion is softened, about 5 minutes. Add the thyme, smoked paprika, and cinnamon and cook until fragrant, about 1 minute. Add the tomatoes, rinse the can with 1½ cups pasta water, and add the water as well. Add the bay leaves and season with salt and red pepper flakes. Simmer until the eggplant is very tender and the sauce is thick and flavorful, about 20 minutes.

3. When the sauce is almost ready, add the rigatoni to the boiling water. When the pasta is al dente, remove it with a spider or small strainer and add directly to the sauce, along with the parsley, reserving the pasta water. Remove the bay leaves. Toss to coat the pasta with the sauce, adding a splash of pasta water if the pasta seems dry. Remove the skillet from the heat, sprinkle with the grated Pecorino Romano, toss, and serve.

SERVES 6

Pesto

Chickpea Flour Ziti with Pesto and String Beans

We removed some of the extra olive oil and cheese and added fat-free chicken broth to keep this pesto lighter than most but still full of fresh basil flavor. Swapping out the pine nuts for almonds also trims calories, because almonds have the lowest calorie count of any nut. For a more traditional flavor, you can use pine nuts, but it will add a few extra calories.

CALORIES PER SERVING:
490

6 cups loosely packed fresh basil leaves

2 ounces skinned almonds, toasted

2 garlic cloves, crushed and peeled

¾ cup low-sodium chicken broth, chilled

¼ cup extra-virgin olive oil

3 ounces freshly grated Grana Padano

Kosher salt

1 pound chickpea flour ziti

4 cups trimmed and halved green beans

1. Bring a large pot of salted water to a boil for pasta. In the work bowl of a food processor, combine the basil, almonds, and garlic. Pulse to make a coarse paste. In a spouted measuring cup, mix together the chicken broth and olive oil. With the machine running, pour in the mixture and process to make an almost-smooth pesto, scraping the sides of the work bowl once or twice to incorporate all of the basil. Scrape the pesto into a serving bowl and stir in the grated Grana Padano. Season with salt.

2. Add the ziti to the boiling water. In the last 5 minutes of cooking time, add the green beans. When the pasta is al dente, drain and reserve 1 cup pasta water. Rinse out the food processor work bowl with ½ cup pasta water to get the last bits of pesto and add to the bowl. Add the hot pasta and green beans to the serving bowl. Toss well to coat with the pesto, adding a splash of pasta water if the pasta seems dry. Serve immediately.

SERVES 6

Spaghetti with Trapanese Pesto

This is a lighter version of the classic Sicilian dish from the town of Trapani. Make sure to use juicy, ripe cherry or grape tomatoes and you'll need very little olive oil to moisten the pasta. To bulk up this dish without adding a lot of extra calories, toss in some sautéed eggplant or zucchini when combining the pasta with the sauce.

CALORIES PER SERVING:
429

1 pint very ripe cherry or grape tomatoes

1 cup loosely packed fresh Italian parsley leaves

1 cup loosely packed fresh basil leaves

⅓ cup almond slivers, toasted

1 garlic clove, crushed and peeled

¼ cup extra-virgin olive oil

Kosher salt

Crushed red pepper flakes

1 pound spaghetti

½ cup freshly grated Grana Padano

1. Bring a large pot of salted water to a boil for pasta. In the work bowl of a food processor, combine the tomatoes, parsley, basil, almonds, and garlic. Process to make a chunky paste, scraping down the sides of the work bowl.

2. With the machine running, pour in the olive oil and process to make an almost-smooth pesto. Scrape the pesto into a large serving bowl and season with salt and red pepper flakes.

3. Meanwhile, add the spaghetti to the boiling water. When the pasta is al dente, remove it with tongs and add directly to the pesto in the serving bowl, reserving the pasta water. Rinse out the food processor work bowl with ½ cup pasta water to get the last bits of pesto and add to the bowl. Sprinkle with the grated Grana Padano. Toss well to coat the pasta with the pesto, adding a splash of pasta water if the pasta seems dry (though you don't want it to be soupy). Serve immediately.

SERVES 6

Bucatini with Broccoli Walnut Pesto

You can vary the nuts (almonds, pine nuts, hazelnuts) in this recipe to suit your tastes, keeping in mind that almonds have the fewest calories. This pesto is also good dolloped into vegetable soup, on a sandwich, or on a pizza.

CALORIES PER SERVING:
481

4 cups lightly packed small broccoli florets

⅓ cup walnut pieces, toasted

1 cup packed fresh Italian parsley leaves

1 cup packed fresh basil leaves

2 garlic cloves, crushed and peeled

⅓ cup low-sodium chicken broth

⅓ cup extra-virgin olive oil

Kosher salt and freshly ground black pepper

¾ cup freshly grated Grana Padano

1 pound bucatini

1. Bring a large pot of salted water to a boil for pasta. Add the broccoli and blanch until bright green, about 2 minutes. Remove with a spider or small strainer to a bowl of ice water. Drain and pat very dry. Return the water to a boil for the pasta.

2. In the work bowl of a food processor, combine the cooked broccoli, walnuts, parsley, basil, and garlic. Process to make a chunky paste, scraping down the sides of the work bowl. With the machine running, pour in the chicken broth and then the olive oil to make an almost-smooth pesto. Scrape the pesto into a large serving bowl and season with salt and pepper. Stir in the grated Grana Padano.

3. Add the bucatini to the boiling water. When the pasta is al dente, remove it with tongs and add directly to the sauce, reserving the pasta water. Rinse out the food processor work bowl with ½ cup pasta water to get the last bits of pesto and drizzle, as needed, into the pasta to moisten. Toss well to coat the pasta with the pesto. Serve immediately.

SERVES 6

Penne with Kale Pesto

Baby kale is tender and has less bitterness than regular kale. It doesn't require cooking, making it perfect for this pesto. The tomato adds both flavor and liquid to the pesto without additional oil.

CALORIES PER SERVING:
425

4 cups loosely packed baby kale

2 cups loosely packed fresh basil leaves

1 medium plum tomato, seeded and chopped (about ¼ cup)

¼ cup pine nuts, toasted

2 cloves garlic, crushed and peeled

Zest and juice of 1 small lemon

¼ cup extra-virgin olive oil

½ cup freshly grated Grana Padano

Kosher salt

1 pound penne

1. Bring a large pot of salted water to a boil for pasta. In the work bowl of a food processor, combine the kale, basil, tomato, pine nuts, garlic, lemon zest, and lemon juice. Pulse to make a coarse paste, scraping down the sides of the bowl. With the processor running, add the olive oil through the feed tube in a steady stream and process to make a smooth pesto, scraping down the sides once or twice. Scrape the pesto into a large serving bowl and stir in the grated cheese. Season with salt to taste.

2. Add the penne to the boiling water. When the pasta is al dente, remove it with a spider or small strainer and add directly to the bowl with the pesto, reserving the pasta water. Rinse out the bowl of the food processor with ½ cup pasta water to get the last bits of pesto and drizzle into the pasta. Toss to coat the pasta with the pesto, adding a splash of pasta water if the pasta seems dry.

SERVES 6

Spaghetti with Beet Pesto

Roasting the beets, rather than boiling them, intensifies their flavor. You can wash and chop the beet greens, if any; sauté and serve as a side or toss in with the pasta. You can roast the beets earlier in the day or even the day before. Once that's done, this dish comes together in the time it takes to cook the pasta.

CALORIES PER SERVING:
429

2 medium beets, unpeeled

Kosher salt and freshly ground black pepper

1 pound spaghetti

⅓ cup almond slivers, toasted

Zest and juice of 1 lemon

2 garlic cloves, crushed and peeled

¼ cup extra-virgin olive oil

¾ cup freshly grated Grana Padano

1 cup fresh Italian parsley leaves, chopped

1. Preheat the oven to 425°F.

2. Bring a large pot of salted water to a boil for pasta. Wrap each beet individually in aluminum foil, sealing tightly. Roast on a sheet pan until tender, about 45 minutes. Let cool until you can peel them. Peel, cut into chunks, and place in the work bowl of a food processor (you will have about 1½ cups of chunked beets). Season with salt and pepper.

3. Add the spaghetti to the boiling water. To the work bowl of the food processor with the beets, add the almonds, lemon zest, lemon juice, and garlic. Pulse to make a chunky paste, scraping down the sides of the work bowl. With the machine running, add the olive oil in a steady stream and process to make a smooth pesto. Scrape into a large serving bowl and stir in the grated Grana Padano and the parsley.

4. When the pasta is al dente, remove it with tongs and add directly to the pesto. Rinse out the food processor work bowl with ½ cup pasta water to get the last bits of pesto and add to the bowl. Toss well to coat the pasta with the pesto until it is an even, bright pink color, adding a splash of pasta water if the pasta seems dry. Serve immediately.

SERVES 6

Gemelli with Parsley, Mint, and Pistachio Pesto

This pesto would also be delicious over grilled fish or tossed with sautéed shrimp or scallops. Pistachios are one of the healthier nuts—they are low in calories and their fiber content makes them more filling, so you eat fewer.

CALORIES PER SERVING:
479

1 pound gemelli

4 cups loosely packed fresh Italian parsley leaves

2 cups loosely packed fresh mint leaves

⅓ cup shelled unsalted pistachios, toasted

1 garlic clove, crushed and peeled

Zest and juice of 1 small orange

6 tablespoons extra-virgin olive oil

Kosher salt and freshly ground black pepper

½ cup freshly grated Grana Padano

1. Bring a large pot of salted water to a boil for pasta. Add the gemelli to the boiling water.

2. While the pasta cooks, in the work bowl of a food processor, combine the parsley, mint, pistachios, garlic, orange zest, and orange juice. Process to make a coarse paste, scraping down the sides of the work bowl. With the machine running, pour in the olive oil and process to make a smooth pesto. Scrape the pesto into a large serving bowl and season with salt and pepper. Stir in the grated Grana Padano.

3. When the pasta is al dente, remove it with tongs and add directly to the bowl, reserving the pasta water. Rinse the food processer work bowl with ½ cup pasta water to get the last bits of pesto and sprinkle over the pasta. Toss to coat the pasta with the pesto, adding a splash of pasta water if the pasta seems dry. Serve immediately.

SERVES 6

Farfalle with Sun-Dried Tomato Pesto

For this sauce, we rehydrate good-quality sun-dried tomatoes and then make a pesto with them and good-quality olive oil, rather than buying the premarinated tomatoes. The flavor is brighter and you get more bang for your buck—more flavor and fewer calories. Save the soaking water to replace some of the oil in the sauce. We add one fresh tomato, for its juice, so we don't have to use as much oil as in a regular pesto.

CALORIES PER SERVING:
469

1 cup packed sun-dried tomatoes

1 ripe plum tomato, seeded and chopped

⅓ cup slivered almonds, toasted

1 garlic clove, crushed and peeled

1 cup loosely packed fresh Italian parsley leaves

1 cup loosely packed fresh basil leaves

⅓ cup extra-virgin olive oil

½ cup freshly grated Grana Padano

Kosher salt and freshly ground black pepper

1 pound farfalle

1. Bring a large pot of salted water to a boil for pasta. Put the sun-dried tomatoes in a bowl and add hot pasta water to cover. Let soak until softened, about 20 minutes, then drain, reserving the soaking water, and chop. (Depending on how dry your tomatoes are, you may need to add hot water halfway through the soaking time.)

2. In the work bowl of a food processor, combine the chopped sun-dried tomatoes, plum tomato, almonds, garlic, parsley, and basil. Process to make a chunky paste, scraping down the sides of the work bowl. With the machine running, add the olive oil in a steady stream to make an almost-smooth pesto. Scrape the pesto into a large serving bowl and stir in the grated Grana Padano. Season with salt and pepper.

3. Add the farfalle to the boiling water. When the pasta is al dente, remove it with a spider or small strainer and add directly to the bowl. Toss well to coat the pasta with the pesto. Add up to ½ cup tomato soaking water if the pasta seems dry and toss again. Serve immediately.

SERVES 6

Linguine with Arugula and Parsley Pesto

This pesto contains no dairy, so it is good for those who are lactose intolerant or just try to steer clear of dairy products. Anchovies add the salty, savory note that the cheese usually provides. The lemon gives the dish a fresh flavor.

CALORIES PER SERVING:
457

1 pound linguine

4 cups loosely packed baby arugula

2 cups loosely packed fresh Italian parsley leaves

⅓ cup walnut pieces, toasted

4 anchovy fillets

2 tablespoons capers in brine, drained

2 garlic cloves, crushed and peeled

Zest and juice of 1 lemon

6 tablespoons extra-virgin olive oil

Kosher salt and freshly ground black pepper

1. Bring a large pot of salted water to a boil for pasta. Add the linguine to the boiling water.

2. While the pasta is cooking, in the work bowl of a food processor, combine the arugula, parsley, walnuts, anchovies, capers, garlic, lemon zest, and lemon juice. Process to make a coarse paste, scraping down the sides of the work bowl. With the machine running, pour in the olive oil and process to make a smooth pesto. Scrape the pesto into a large serving bowl and season with salt and lots of freshly ground black pepper.

3. When the pasta is al dente, remove it with tongs and add directly to the bowl, reserving the pasta water. Rinse out the food processor work bowl with ½ cup pasta water to get the last bits of pesto and sprinkle over the pasta. Toss well to coat the pasta with the pesto, adding a splash of pasta water if the pasta seems dry. Serve immediately.

SERVES 6

Gemelli with Pea and Mint Pesto

The flavor of this pesto is especially bright when made with the new sweet peas of spring. Any other time of year, frozen baby peas are a good substitute. Rinse the peas to remove some of the sodium added during the freezing process. Because peas are starchy, this pesto comes out thicker than most, so don't be afraid to add a little more pasta water than usual when dressing the pasta.

CALORIES PER SERVING:
455

1 (10-ounce) box frozen peas or 1½ cups fresh shelled peas

1 cup loosely packed fresh Italian parsley leaves

1 cup loosely packed fresh mint leaves

3 tablespoons pine nuts, toasted

1 garlic clove, crushed and peeled

¼ cup extra-virgin olive oil

½ cup freshly grated Grana Padano

Kosher salt and freshly ground black pepper

1 pound gemelli

I. Bring a large pot of salted water to a boil for pasta. Bring a small pot of salted water to a boil for the peas. Prepare a medium bowl with ice water for the peas. When the water is boiling, add the peas to the small saucepan and blanch until just tender, about 3 minutes for frozen, 5 minutes for fresh. Drain and plunge directly into the ice water to cool and preserve the bright green color. Drain and pat dry.

2. In the work bowl of a food processor, combine the peas, parsley, mint, pine nuts, and garlic. Process to make a coarse paste, scraping down the sides of the work bowl. With the machine running, pour in the olive oil and process to make a smooth, thick pesto. Add ½ cup pasta water and process again until smooth. Scrape the pesto into a large serving bowl and stir in the grated Grana Padano. Season with salt and lots of freshly ground black pepper.

3. Add the gemelli to the boiling water. When the pasta is al dente, remove it with a spider or small strainer and add directly to the bowl, reserving the pasta water. Rinse out the food processor work bowl with ½ cup pasta water to get the last bits of pesto and sprinkle over the pasta. Toss well to coat the pasta with the pesto, adding a splash of pasta water if the pasta seems dry. Serve immediately.

SERVES 6

Pesce

—

Fish

Linguine with Shrimp and Lemon

Lemon and cream are natural partners to seafood. You could also make this dish with an equal amount of scallops, crab, or calamari.

CALORIES PER SERVING: 410

2 tablespoons extra-virgin olive oil

1 pound large shrimp, peeled and deveined, tails removed, and shrimp halved lengthwise

Kosher salt

2 cups chopped scallions

3 tablespoons capers in brine, drained

Crushed red pepper flakes

Zest and juice of 1 large lemon

½ cup dry white wine

¼ cup heavy cream

1 cup fresh Italian parsley leaves, chopped

1 pound linguine

1. Bring a large pot of salted water to a boil for pasta. In a large skillet over medium-high heat, add 1 tablespoon of the olive oil. Season the shrimp with salt. When the oil is hot, add the shrimp and cook just until they begin to curl and turn white, 2 to 3 minutes. Remove to a plate.

2. Return the skillet to the heat and add the remaining 1 tablespoon olive oil. Add the scallions and cook until wilted, about 3 minutes. Add the capers and red pepper flakes and cook until they begin to sizzle, about 1 minute. Add the lemon zest, lemon juice, and white wine and simmer until reduced by half, about 2 minutes. Add 1 cup pasta water and the cream and simmer while you cook the pasta. Add the shrimp and parsley to the sauce for the last 3 minutes of cooking time.

3. Add the linguine to the boiling water. When the sauce is ready and the pasta is al dente, remove the pasta with tongs and add directly to the sauce, reserving the pasta water. Toss to coat the pasta with the sauce, adding a splash of pasta water if the pasta seems dry. Serve immediately.

SERVES 6

Shells with Lentils and Shrimp

Using quality canned (organic, if possible) lentils makes this dish quick and easy. Quality is important because a better product is more flavorful, and many organic canned foods are now packaged in cans that do not contain bisphenol A (BPA). Lentils, a good source of cholesterol-lowering fiber, also keep blood sugar from rising, keeping you satiated longer. If you have extra time, simmer the shells and tails from the shrimp in the broth for 15 minutes to add flavor. Strain and use as directed in the recipe.

CALORIES PER SERVING:
469

3 tablespoons extra-virgin olive oil

12 ounces large shrimp, peeled and deveined, tails removed, and shrimp halved lengthwise

Kosher salt

1 medium onion, chopped (about 1 cup)

1 large carrot, chopped (about 1½ cups)

1 medium zucchini, chopped (about 1½ cups)

Crushed red pepper flakes

2 teaspoons fresh thyme leaves, chopped

3 garlic cloves, thinly sliced

1 (15-ounce) can brown lentils, rinsed and drained

½ cup dry white wine

2 cups low-sodium chicken broth

2 fresh bay leaves

1 cup fresh Italian parsley leaves, chopped

1 pound medium shells

1. Bring a large pot of salted water to a boil for pasta. In a large skillet over medium-high heat, add 1 tablespoon of the olive oil. Season the shrimp with salt. When the oil is hot, add the shrimp and cook just until the shrimp curl and start to turn white, 2 to 3 minutes. Remove to a plate.

2. Return the skillet to the heat and reduce the heat to medium. Add the remaining 2 tablespoons olive oil. Add the onion, carrot, and zucchini and cook until just softened, about 12 minutes. Season with salt and red pepper flakes and add the thyme and garlic. Cook until fragrant, about 1 minute. Add the drained lentils and stir to combine. Add the white wine and bring to a simmer. Add the chicken broth and bay leaves. Bring to a simmer and cook until the vegetables are tender and the lentils just begin to break down and thicken the sauce, about 15 minutes. Add the shrimp and parsley in the last few minutes of cooking time, just to finish cooking the shrimp and heat them through. Remove the bay leaves.

3. Add the shells to the boiling water. When the sauce is ready and the pasta is al dente, remove the pasta with a spider or small strainer and add directly to the sauce, reserving the pasta water. Toss to coat the pasta in the sauce, adding a splash of pasta water if the pasta seems dry. Serve immediately.

SERVES 6

Fettuccine with Roasted Peppers and Shrimp

This sauce is like a deconstructed version of a Spanish romesco sauce, with lots of roasted bell peppers, onion, almonds, garlic, and spices.

CALORIES PER SERVING: 446

2 medium red bell peppers

3 tablespoons extra-virgin olive oil

⅓ cup panko bread crumbs

⅓ cup slivered almonds, coarsely chopped

Kosher salt

½ cup fresh Italian parsley leaves, chopped

12 ounces large shrimp, peeled and deveined, tails removed, and shrimp halved lengthwise

1 medium onion, sliced (about 1 cup)

4 garlic cloves, thinly sliced

2 tablespoons tomato paste

1 teaspoon smoked paprika

Crushed red pepper flakes

½ cup dry white wine

1 pound fettuccine

1. Bring a large pot of salted water to a boil for pasta. Turn on flame and char the peppers on all sides, turning frequently, 8 to 10 minutes. Put the peppers in a medium bowl and cover tightly with plastic wrap. Let steam until cooled. Peel the skin from the peppers. Remove the stems and seeds and cut the peppers into ¼-inch-thick slices.

2. In a small skillet over medium heat, add 2 teaspoons of the olive oil. When the oil is hot, add the panko and almonds. Cook and toss until golden and toasted, 3 to 4 minutes. Scrape into a small bowl, season with salt, and let cool. Stir in the parsley.

3. In a large skillet over medium-high heat, add 1 tablespoon of the remaining olive oil. Season the shrimp with salt. When the oil is hot, add the shrimp and cook just until they begin to curl and turn white, 2 to 3 minutes. Remove to a plate.

4. Return the skillet to medium heat and add the remaining 1 tablespoon and 2 teaspoons olive oil. When the oil is hot, add the onion and cook until wilted, about 5 minutes. Add the bell peppers and garlic and cook until the peppers are soft, about 3 minutes. Make a space in the pan and add the tomato paste. Cook, stirring in that spot, until the tomato paste toasts and darkens a shade or two, about 2 minutes. Stir into the onion and peppers. Sprinkle with the paprika and season with salt and red pepper flakes. Pour in the white wine, bring to a simmer, and cook until reduced by half, about 2 minutes. Add 1 cup pasta water and let simmer while you cook the pasta.

5. Meanwhile, add the fettuccine to the boiling water. When the sauce is ready, add back the shrimp and the juices from the plate. When the pasta is al dente, remove it with tongs and add directly to the sauce, reserving the pasta water. Stir about half of the almond mixture into the sauce and toss to coat the pasta with the sauce, adding a splash of pasta water if the pasta seems dry. Serve immediately in warmed pasta bowls with the remaining crumbs sprinkled over the top.

SERVES 6

Orecchiette with Shrimp, Cauliflower, and Red Pepper Oil

Two types of chiles, dried and fresh, give an intense kick to this oil. You can double or triple the oil recipe and use it in other pastas or as a final drizzle on a pasta and bean soup or grilled fish. The oil will keep in the fridge for about a week.

Fresno chiles look similar to red jalapeños but are a little spicier and have a hint of fruitiness.

CALORIES PER SERVING:
445

¼ cup extra-virgin olive oil

½ teaspoon crushed red pepper flakes, plus more for garnish

2 Fresno chiles, cut in thin rings (seeding is optional; leave them in for maximum heat)

12 ounces large shrimp, peeled and deveined, tails removed, and shrimp halved lengthwise

Kosher salt

1 medium head cauliflower, cut into small florets, tender leaves coarsely chopped (about 8 cups)

2 cups chopped scallions

½ cup dry white wine

1 pound orecchiette

1 cup fresh Italian parsley leaves, chopped

1. Bring a large pot of salted water to a boil for pasta. In a small skillet, heat the oil over low heat. Add the red pepper flakes and sliced Fresno chiles. Let the chiles sizzle gently until the Fresnos are very tender, about 8 minutes, but don't let anything burn. Let cool completely and strain, pressing on the solids. Discard the solids.

2. In a large skillet over medium-high heat, add 1 tablespoon of the pepper oil. Season the shrimp with salt and add to the skillet. Cook just until the shrimp curl and are no longer pink, about 3 minutes. Remove to a plate.

3. In the same skillet, over medium-high heat, add 2 tablespoons of the pepper oil. When the oil is hot, add the cauliflower, toss to coat in the oil, and season with salt. Toss and cook until the cauliflower begins to brown on the edges, about 5 minutes. Add the scallions and cook until wilted, about 3 minutes. Add the white wine and cook until reduced by half, about 2 minutes. Add 1 cup pasta water, cover, and cook until cauliflower is very tender, about 7 minutes. Uncover and then increase the heat to reduce away the water and let the cauliflower caramelize all over, about 4 minutes.

4. Meanwhile, add the orecchiette to the boiling water. When the pasta is al dente and the cauliflower is caramelized, add ½ cup pasta water, the parsley, and the shrimp to the cauliflower and bring to a simmer. Remove the pasta with a spider or small strainer and add directly to the sauce, reserving the pasta water. Drizzle with the remaining tablespoon of pepper oil. Toss and serve, garnishing with more red pepper flakes if a final burst of heat is desired.

SERVES 6

Linguine with Spicy Mussels, White Wine, and Garlic Sauce

Prince Edward Island mussels are a reliable farmed variety of mussels and usually arrive very clean, so you need to give them only a quick scrub and check for stray beards. For a more finished look to this dish, you can pluck the mussels from the shells once they steam open in the pot.

CALORIES PER SERVING:
463

2 tablespoons extra-virgin olive oil

2 ounces pancetta, chopped

2 cups chopped scallions

6 garlic cloves, thinly sliced

4 hot pickled cherry peppers, stemmed, seeded (if desired), and sliced, plus 2 tablespoons brine from the jar

¾ cup dry white wine

2 pounds mussels

6 cups loosely packed baby kale

Kosher salt

1 pound linguine

1 cup fresh Italian parsley leaves, chopped

1. Bring a large pot of salted water to a boil for pasta. Heat a large Dutch oven over medium heat. Add the olive oil. When the oil is hot, add the pancetta and cook until the fat is rendered, about 4 minutes. Add the scallions and cook until wilted, about 3 minutes. Add the garlic and cherry peppers and let sizzle a minute. Add the white wine and brine from the pepper jar. Bring to a simmer, add the mussels and kale, and cover. Simmer until all of the mussels open, about 4 minutes.

2. Meanwhile, add the linguine to the boiling water. Discard any mussels that haven't opened and add the parsley to the sauce. When the pasta is al dente, remove it with tongs and add directly to the sauce, reserving the pasta water. Toss to coat the pasta with the sauce, adding a splash of pasta water if the pasta seems dry. Serve immediately.

SERVES 6

Spaghetti alle Vongole

For the most flavor, toast the fennel seeds and grind them yourself in a spice grinder. Including fennel (both fresh and seeds) isn't typical in this dish, but it adds a lot of flavor without more calories, so you can use less oil than usual.

CALORIES PER SERVING:
402

3 tablespoons extra-virgin olive oil

2 medium shallots, chopped (about ¼ cup)

1 small fennel bulb, cored and sliced (about 2 cups), plus ½ cup fronds, chopped

4 garlic cloves, thinly sliced

2 anchovy fillets

Kosher salt

Crushed red pepper flakes

½ teaspoon ground fennel seeds

¾ cup dry white wine

3 dozen Manila clams or other small clams

Zest of 1 small lemon

1 pound spaghetti

1 cup fresh Italian parsley leaves, chopped

I. Bring a large pot of salted water to a boil for pasta. In a large Dutch oven over medium heat, add 2 tablespoons of the olive oil. When the oil is hot, add the shallots and sliced fennel and cook until very tender, about 10 minutes.

2. Add the garlic and anchovies. Cook and stir with a wooden spoon until the anchovies dissolve into the oil, about 2 minutes. Season with salt and red pepper flakes and sprinkle with the ground fennel. Add the white wine, bring to a boil, and add the clams and lemon zest. Cover and cook until all of the clams just open (discard any that don't), 6 to 8 minutes. Uncover and boil for 1 minute to reduce the sauce slightly.

3. Meanwhile, add the spaghetti to the boiling water. When the pasta is al dente, remove it with tongs and add directly to the sauce, reserving the pasta water. Add the parsley and chopped fennel fronds. Drizzle with the remaining 1 tablespoon olive oil and toss to coat the pasta with the sauce, adding a splash of pasta water if the pasta seems dry. Serve immediately.

SERVES 6

Casarecce with Corn and Lobster

Two 1½-pound lobsters will yield about 2½ cups lobster meat. Cooking the pasta in the lobster cooking water will lend a subtle taste of the sea to the dish. You could also add the corn cobs to the cooking water to further incorporate that flavor as well.

Casarecce are tube-shaped pasta, rolled like a scroll. You can substitute gemelli.

CALORIES PER SERVING:
490

2 (1½-pound) lobsters

2 cups low-sodium chicken broth

3 tablespoons extra-virgin olive oil

2 ounces pancetta, diced

2 celery stalks, chopped (about 1 cup), plus ½ cup tender leaves

2 cups chopped scallions

4 ears of corn, kernels removed from the cobs (about 2 cups)

2 teaspoons fresh thyme leaves, chopped

Kosher salt

Crushed red pepper flakes

½ cup dry white wine

1 pound casarecce

1 cup fresh basil leaves, chopped

1 cup fresh Italian parsley leaves, chopped

1. Bring a very large pot of salted water to a boil. Once it's boiling, add the lobsters. Cover and boil until the lobsters are cooked through, about 10 to 12 minutes. Rinse under cold water and let cool. Return the water to a boil for the pasta.

2. Remove the tiny legs from the bodies of the lobsters and put them in a small saucepan with the chicken broth. Simmer while you prepare the other ingredients, then strain, discarding the lobster parts.

3. Remove the lobster meat from the tail and large claws and cut into ½-inch chunks.

4. In a large skillet over medium heat, add 2 tablespoons of the olive oil. When the oil is hot, add the pancetta and cook until the fat is rendered, about 4 minutes. Add the chopped celery and cook until it begins to soften, about 5 minutes. Add the scallions and cook until wilted, about 3 minutes. Add the corn kernels and toss to coat in the oil. Add the thyme and season with salt and red pepper flakes. Add the white wine, bring to a simmer, and cook until reduced by half, about 3 minutes. Add the strained chicken broth and let simmer while you cook the pasta.

5. Add the casarecce to the lobster cooking water. When the sauce is ready and the pasta is al dente, add the lobster meat, basil, and parsley to the sauce. Remove the pasta with a spider or small strainer and add directly to the sauce, reserving the pasta water. Toss to coat the pasta with the sauce, adding a splash of pasta water if the pasta seems dry. Drizzle with the remaining 1 tablespoon olive oil. Serve immediately.

SERVES 6

Orecchiette with Crab and Artichokes

This simple, fresh pasta is all about the crab, so make sure you purchase fresh lump crab-meat from your fishmonger. Before using, spread it out on a baking sheet and gently pick through it for any stray shells. This dish comes together quickly, so prep all of your ingredients in advance and start cooking the pasta at the same time you start the sauce.

CALORIES PER SERVING:
439

1 pound orecchiette

3 tablespoons extra-virgin olive oil

2 cups chopped scallions

8 ounces (after draining) marinated artichoke quarters, patted dry and coarsely chopped

1 pound lump crabmeat

Zest and juice of 1 medium lemon

Kosher salt

Crushed red pepper flakes

½ cup fresh Italian parsley leaves, chopped

¼ cup fresh mint leaves, chopped

I. Bring a large pot of salted water to a boil for pasta. Add the orecchiette to the boiling water.

2. In a large skillet over medium-high heat, add the olive oil and scallions. Cook until wilted, about 3 minutes. Add the artichokes and cook until they just begin to brown on the edges, about 3 minutes. Add the crabmeat and toss just until heated through, about 2 minutes. Add the lemon zest and season with salt and red pepper flakes. Add the lemon juice and 1 cup pasta water and simmer while the pasta cooks.

3. When the pasta is al dente, dump the sauce into a serving bowl. Remove the pasta with a spider or small strainer and add directly to the sauce, along with the parsley and mint. Toss to coat the pasta with the sauce and serve immediately.

SERVES 6

Rotini with Tuna Puttanesca

You're used to seeing fresh tuna cooked rare, but here we cook it all the way through and it soaks up the flavor of the sauce. Make sure it doesn't overcook, though—you want it just cooked through and still moist in the center.

CALORIES PER SERVING:
468

3 tablespoons extra-virgin olive oil

12 ounces tuna steak, cut into ½-inch chunks

Kosher salt

1 cup chopped scallions

3 garlic cloves, thinly sliced

½ cup pitted black Italian olives (such as Gaeta), coarsely chopped (about 20)

¼ cup capers in brine, drained

4 anchovy fillets

Crushed red pepper flakes

1 (28-ounce) can whole San Marzano tomatoes, crushed by hand

½ teaspoon dried oregano, preferably Sicilian oregano on the branch

1 pound rotini

1 cup fresh basil leaves, chopped

1 cup fresh Italian parsley leaves, chopped

1. Bring a large pot of salted water to a boil for pasta. In a large skillet over medium-high heat, add 1 tablespoon of the olive oil. Pat the tuna dry and season with salt. Brown the tuna all over (but don't cook through yet), 2 to 3 minutes. Remove to a plate.

2. Return the skillet to the heat and add the remaining 2 tablespoons olive oil. When the oil is hot, add the scallions and cook until wilted, about 3 minutes. Add the garlic and let sizzle until golden on the edges, about 1 minute. Add the olives, capers, and anchovies. Cook and stir with a wooden spoon until the anchovies dissolve into the oil, about 2 minutes. Season with salt and red pepper flakes.

3. Add the tomatoes and 1 cup pasta water. Crumble in the oregano. Bring to a simmer and cook until thick and flavorful, about 20 minutes, adding the tuna and juices from the plate in the last 3 minutes of cooking time.

4. When the sauce is almost ready, add the rotini to the boiling water. When the pasta is al dente, remove it with a spider or small strainer and add directly to the sauce, reserving the pasta water. Add the basil and parsley. Toss to coat the pasta with the sauce, adding a splash of pasta water if the pasta seems dry. Serve immediately.

SERVES 6

Campanelle with Swordfish, Bell Peppers, and Capers

Trim away any dark spots (which are from the fish's bloodline) on the swordfish before cutting it into cubes. If you can't get swordfish, use another firm fish, like halibut or monkfish. Swordfish is really rich in nutrients and is very low in calories per serving.

CALORIES PER SERVING:
466

3 tablespoons extra-virgin olive oil

1 pound skinless swordfish, cut into ½-inch chunks

Kosher salt

2 small red, orange, or yellow bell peppers, cut into ½-inch chunks (about 2½ cups)

1 cup chopped scallions

4 garlic cloves, thinly sliced

3 tablespoons capers in brine, drained

2 hot pickled cherry peppers, stemmed, seeded, and sliced, plus 2 tablespoons brine from the jar

2 tablespoons tomato paste

¾ cup dry white wine

1 pound campanelle

½ cup fresh Italian parsley leaves, chopped

1. Bring a large pot of salted water to a boil for pasta. In a large skillet over medium-high heat, add 2 tablespoons of the olive oil. Pat the swordfish dry and season with salt. When the oil is hot, brown the swordfish cubes on all sides (but they don't need to be cooked through at this point), 2 to 3 minutes. Remove to a plate.

2. In the same skillet, add the bell pepper chunks and cook until just softened and browned on the edges, about 4 minutes. Add the scallions and cook until wilted, about 3 minutes. Add the garlic, capers, and sliced cherry peppers and cook until sizzling, about 1 minute. Season with salt. Make a space in the pan and add the tomato paste. Let cook, stirring in that spot, until the tomato paste toasts and darkens a shade or two, about 2 minutes. Stir into the vegetables. Add the white wine and brine from the jar and bring to a simmer. Cook until reduced by half, about 2 minutes. Add 1 cup pasta water and simmer while you cook the pasta.

3. Add the campanelle to the boiling water. When the pasta is about halfway done, add the swordfish and juices from the plate to the sauce and continue to simmer to cook the swordfish all the way through. When the sauce is ready and the pasta is al dente, remove the pasta with a spider or small strainer and add directly to the sauce, reserving the pasta water. Add the parsley, drizzle with the remaining 1 tablespoon olive oil, and toss to coat the pasta with the sauce, adding a splash of pasta water if the pasta seems dry. Serve immediately.

SERVES 6

Mostaccioli with Asparagus and Smoked Salmon

A little low-fat cream cheese melts into this sauce, providing a creaminess that perfectly complements the salmon without adding a lot of calories or fat. Add the salmon at the very end—you don't want to cook it, just heat it through. The salmon contributes an incredible amount of flavor, and it would be difficult to notice the difference between a regular and low-fat cream cheese.

CALORIES PER SERVING:
421

1 large bunch asparagus (about 30 spears)

2 tablespoons extra-virgin olive oil

2 cups chopped scallions

Kosher salt and freshly ground black pepper

Zest and juice of 1 small lemon

½ cup dry white wine

1 pound mostaccioli

2 ounces low-fat (Neufchâtel) cream cheese, at room temperature

8 ounces sliced smoked salmon, cut into strips

½ cup fresh Italian parsley leaves, chopped

½ cup chopped fresh chives

1. Bring a large pot of salted water to a boil for pasta. Snap off the woody lower stems of the asparagus and peel the lower half of the remaining stems. Cut the asparagus on the bias into pieces about the same length as the pasta.

2. In a large skillet over medium-high heat, add the olive oil. When the oil is hot, add the asparagus and cook and toss until bright green, about 3 minutes. Add the scallions and cook until wilted, about 3 minutes. Season with salt and pepper. Add the lemon zest, lemon juice, and white wine and bring to a simmer. Cook until the wine is reduced to a glaze and toss to coat the asparagus in the glaze, letting it caramelize a little, about 3 minutes. Add 1 cup pasta water and simmer until the asparagus is tender, about 4 minutes.

3. Meanwhile, add the mostaccioli to the boiling water. When the pasta is almost al dente, whisk the cream cheese into the sauce and bring just to a simmer. Add the salmon, parsley, and chives and simmer just to heat through. When the pasta is al dente, remove it with a spider or small strainer and add directly to the sauce, reserving the pasta water. Toss to coat the pasta with the sauce, adding a splash of pasta water if the pasta seems dry. Serve immediately.

SERVES 6

Penne with Creamy Salmon and Green Olive Sauce

Take care not to overcook the salmon when you are searing it, because it will continue cooking in the sauce. While mustard isn't a traditional ingredient in pasta sauces, it works here to add a little heat to balance out the creaminess of the sauce.

CALORIES PER SERVING:
426

1 (12-ounce) center-cut skinless wild salmon fillet

Kosher salt

2 tablespoons extra-virgin olive oil

2 medium leeks, white and light green parts, sliced (about 1 cup)

¼ cup slivered Italian green olives, such as Cerignola (about 10 olives)

2 tablespoons capers in brine, drained

½ cup dry white wine

1 cup low-sodium chicken broth

¼ cup heavy cream

1 pound penne

2 teaspoons Dijon mustard

¼ cup chopped fresh chives

¼ cup fresh Italian parsley leaves, chopped

1. Bring a large pot of salted water to a boil for pasta. Season the salmon with salt. In a large nonstick skillet over medium-high heat, add the olive oil. When the oil is hot, add the salmon and sear until just cooked through, 3 to 4 minutes per side. Remove to a plate, let cool, and flake with your fingers or a fork.

2. Reduce the heat under the skillet to medium and add the leeks. Cook until softened, about 5 minutes. Increase the heat to medium-high and add the olives and capers. Let them sizzle a minute, then add the white wine and cook until reduced to a glaze, about 1 minute. Add the chicken broth and cream and bring to a simmer while you cook the pasta.

3. Add the penne to the boiling water. When the pasta is al dente, whisk the mustard into the sauce and add the flaked salmon, the chives, and parsley. Remove the pasta with a spider or small strainer and add directly to the sauce, reserving the pasta water. Toss to coat the pasta in the sauce, adding a splash of pasta water if the pasta seems dry. Serve immediately.

SERVES 6

Farfalle with Tuna, Marinated Artichokes, Olives, and Peppers

Tuna packed in water can sometimes, paradoxically, be dry. Canned tuna should be firm but flaky, and when it's accompanied by great flavor enhancers such as olives and basil, you won't even notice that it was not packed in oil, saving quite a few calories. The tongol and albacore varieties of tuna seem to be most flavorful when packed in water. To cut more calories, look for artichokes marinated in brine rather than olive oil and roast your own bell pepper rather than using oil-packed ones from the deli.

CALORIES PER SERVING:
476

1 large red bell pepper

¼ cup extra-virgin olive oil

1 cup chopped scallions

3 garlic cloves, thinly sliced

8 ounces (after draining) marinated artichoke quarters, patted dry and coarsely chopped

½ cup pitted green Italian olives (such as Castelvetrano), slivered (about 20)

Kosher salt

Crushed red pepper flakes

½ cup dry white wine

2 (5-ounce) cans white tuna packed in water, drained

1 pound farfalle

1 cup fresh basil leaves, chopped

1 cup fresh Italian parsley leaves, chopped

1. Bring a large pot of salted water to a boil for pasta. Turn on the flame on the stove-top burner and char the bell pepper on all sides, turning frequently, 8 to 10 minutes. Put the pepper in a medium bowl and cover tightly with plastic wrap. Let steam until cooled. Peel the skin from the pepper. Remove the stem and seeds and slice the pepper into ¼-inch-thick slices.

2. In a large skillet over medium heat, heat the olive oil. When the oil is hot, add the scallions and cook until wilted, about 3 minutes. Add the garlic and cook until fragrant, about 1 minute. Add the artichoke quarters, olives, and red pepper slices. Season with salt and red pepper flakes and cook until the artichokes are browned on the edges, about 5 minutes. Add the white wine and cook until reduced by half, about 2 minutes. Crumble in the tuna and add 1 cup pasta water. Simmer and let reduce by half while you cook the pasta.

3. Add the farfalle to the boiling water. When the sauce is ready and the pasta is al dente, add the basil and parsley. Remove the pasta with a spider or small strainer and add directly to the sauce, reserving the pasta water. Toss to coat the pasta with the sauce, adding a splash of pasta water if the pasta seems dry. Serve immediately.

SERVES 6

Bucatini con le Sarde

Sardines are one of the most concentrated sources of omega-3 fatty acids and one of our healthiest foods, particularly when they are packed in water. Named after the island of Sardinia where schools of this fish swim, sardines are being enjoyed more and more, particularly in light of recent concerns with regard to fish and mercury. Sardines, on the bottom of the fish food chain, do not eat other fish; they eat mainly plankton. Since fresh sardines are quite perishable, they are usually found canned. Always look at the expiration date on the can to make sure the sardines are safe. You can also use fresh sardines in this dish, but high-quality imported, canned sardines are easier and faster. If you use fresh ones, have your fishmonger fillet them and remove the heads for you. Brown fresh sardines before the onion and fennel, then remove them from the skillet and add them back when you'd add the canned ones.

CALORIES PER SERVING:
475

¼ cup golden raisins

½ teaspoon saffron threads

3 tablespoons extra-virgin olive oil

½ cup panko bread crumbs

½ cup fresh Italian parsley leaves, chopped

Kosher salt

1 large onion, sliced (about 1½ cups)

1 large fennel bulb, cored and thinly sliced (about 3 cups), plus ½ cup fronds, chopped

Crushed red pepper flakes

4 anchovy fillets

½ teaspoon ground fennel seeds

l. Bring a large pot of salted water to a boil for pasta. Put the raisins and saffron in a small bowl and add 1 cup hot pasta water. In a small skillet over medium heat, heat 1 tablespoon of the olive oil. Add the bread crumbs. Toss and cook until the crumbs are crisp and golden, 5 to 6 minutes. Scrape into a small bowl. Stir in half of the parsley and season with salt.

2. In a large skillet over medium heat, add the remaining 2 tablespoons olive oil. When the oil is hot, add the onion and sliced fennel and toss to coat in the oil. Add about 1 cup pasta water and simmer gently until both are tender, about 1 minute. Increase the heat to reduce away the water and cook until the onion and fennel are golden, about 5 minutes. Season with salt and red pepper flakes and add the anchovies and ground fennel. Cook until fragrant, about 1 minute.

3. Add the raisins in the saffron water and bring to a simmer. Cook until reduced by half, about 4 minutes. Add the sardines and pine nuts and simmer gently while you cook the pasta, taking care not to break up the sardines too much.

4. Meanwhile, add the bucatini to the boiling water. When the sauce is ready and the pasta is al dente, remove the pasta with tongs and add

2 (3.5-ounce) cans sardine fillets, in spring water, drained and dried

¼ cup pine nuts, toasted and coarsely chopped

1 pound bucatini

directly to the sauce, reserving the pasta water. Add the remaining parsley and chopped fennel fronds and toss to coat the pasta in the sauce, adding more pasta water if the pasta seems dry. Serve in warmed pasta bowls, with the toasted bread crumbs on top.

SERVES 6

Pasta in Modi Diversi

Pasta Done Different Ways

Baked Rigatoni with Creamy Mushrooms and Squash

The combination of mushrooms and butternut squash is well suited for fall, but you can substitute other roasted vegetables in this dish, according to the season. The white sauce is a lower-calorie and lower-fat version of the classic besciamella.

CALORIES PER SERVING: 494

1 pound mixed mushrooms (such as button, cremini, shiitake, oyster, chanterelle, or porcini), thickly sliced (about 6 cups)

1 tablespoon extra-virgin olive oil

Kosher salt

1 small butternut squash, peeled and cut into ½-inch cubes (about 3 cups)

1 tablespoon fresh thyme leaves, chopped

2 tablespoons unsalted butter

3 tablespoons all-purpose flour

2 cups 1% low-fat milk

1 cup low-sodium chicken broth

1 fresh bay leaf

Pinch of freshly grated nutmeg

Crushed red pepper flakes

1 pound rigatoni

1 cup shredded low-moisture part-skim mozzarella

¼ cup freshly grated Grana Padano

1. Preheat the oven to 450°F with two sheet pans on the top and bottom racks.

2. Bring a large pot of salted water to a boil for pasta. In a large bowl, toss the mushrooms with ½ tablespoon of the olive oil and season with salt. Spread on one of the preheated pans. Repeat with the squash and the remaining ½ tablespoon olive oil and season with salt and the thyme. Spread on the second sheet pan and roast both until browned and tender, stirring and switching the pans from top to bottom halfway through the cooking time, about 20 minutes in all.

3. Meanwhile, in a medium saucepan over medium heat, melt the butter. When the butter is melted, whisk in the flour to make a smooth paste. Let cook for 2 minutes to remove the raw flour smell, then whisk in the milk and chicken broth. Add the bay leaf and nutmeg and season with salt and red pepper flakes. Simmer, stirring occasionally, until thickened, about 10 minutes. Discard the bay leaf.

4. Add the rigatoni to the boiling water. When the pasta is very al dente, several minutes shy of the package cooking time, drain and rinse. In a small bowl, toss the mozzarella and Grana Padano together. In a large bowl, combine the pasta, white sauce, and roasted vegetables and season with salt. Toss to coat the pasta with the sauce.

5. Pour into a 13-by-9-inch ceramic or glass baking dish. Sprinkle with the grated cheese mixture. Bake until the sauce is bubbly on the edges and the top is browned, 15 to 17 minutes. Let rest for 5 minutes before serving.

SERVES 6

Vegetable Lasagna

This recipe, unlike others in this book, serves eight, because we make it in a 13-by-9-inch dish, but lasagna is good for a large group. Also, lasagna can be made ahead, covered, and baked right before serving, which makes it especially easy for entertaining.

CALORIES PER SERVING:
403

3 tablespoons extra-virgin olive oil

3 garlic cloves, sliced

Kosher salt

Crushed red pepper flakes

1 (28-ounce) can whole San Marzano tomatoes, crushed by hand

1 cup fresh basil leaves, chopped

2 medium zucchini, sliced into ½-inch-thick rounds (about 2½ cups)

1 small Italian eggplant, cut into ½-inch-thick cubes (about 2 cups)

1 medium yellow bell pepper, cut into ½-inch-thick strips

1 small onion, cut into ½-inch-thick slices

12 lasagna noodles (approximately 8 by 3½ inches)

1½ cups part-skim ricotta

1 large egg

1. Preheat the oven to 450°F with two sheet pans on the top and bottom racks.

2. Bring a large pot of salted water to a boil for pasta. For the sauce, in a large skillet over medium heat, add 1 tablespoon of the olive oil. When the oil is hot, add the garlic and let sizzle until just golden on the edges, about 1 minute. Season with salt and red pepper flakes. Add the tomatoes and 2½ cups water. Bring to a simmer and cook until slightly thickened (this should be a little looser than most tomato sauces), about 10 minutes. Stir in the basil and keep warm.

3. In a large bowl, toss the zucchini and eggplant with 1 tablespoon of the olive oil. Season with salt. Spread the mixture on one of the preheated sheet pans and return the pan to the oven. In the same bowl, toss the bell pepper and onion with the remaining 1 tablespoon olive oil and season with salt. Spread the mixture on the other sheet pan. Roast the vegetables, rotating the sheets from top to bottom once, until tender and golden, about 18 minutes for the zucchini and eggplant and 15 minutes for the onion and pepper.

4. Meanwhile, add the lasagna noodles to the boiling water. When the pasta is very al dente, drain and cool under cold running water. Pat dry on kitchen towels. In a medium bowl, stir together the ricotta and egg. In another bowl, toss together the grated mozzarella and Grana Padano.

5. Reduce the oven temperature to 425°F. To assemble, spread about ¾ cup sauce in the bottom of a 13-by-9-inch glass or ceramic baking dish. Add a layer of lasagna noodles, patching any broken ones. Add half of the roasted vegetables, half of the ricotta mixture, and 1¼ cups sauce. Sprinkle with one-third of the grated cheese mixture. Top with noodles and

2 cups shredded part-skim low-moisture mozzarella

½ cup freshly grated Grana Padano

repeat the same layering again. Top with a final layer of noodles. Spread with the remaining sauce and sprinkle with the remaining grated cheese. Bake until the sauce is bubbly on the edges and the top is browned, about 25 minutes. Let stand for 15 minutes before cutting the lasagna into squares and serving.

SERVES 8

Stuffed Shells with Roasted Vegetables

This is a good dish to make ahead. It can be assembled and refrigerated up to a day ahead; just let it sit at room temperature for thirty minutes before baking. Bulking up on the vegetables in the stuffing saves calories, using less ricotta. The mixing of ricotta with cottage cheese also lowers the calories.

CALORIES PER SERVING:
462

3 tablespoons extra-virgin olive oil

3 garlic cloves, thinly sliced

Crushed red pepper flakes

1 (28-ounce) can whole San Marzano tomatoes, crushed by hand

1 cup fresh basil leaves, chopped

Kosher salt

8 ounces mixed mushrooms, cut into ½-inch chunks (4 cups)

2 small zucchini, cut into ½-inch chunks (about 4 cups)

1 medium red bell pepper, seeded and cut into ½-inch chunks

1 cup part-skim ricotta cheese

½ cup 1% low-fat cottage cheese

¾ cup freshly grated Grana Padano

1 cup shredded low-moisture part-skim mozzarella

30 jumbo pasta shells (about one 12-ounce box)

I. Preheat the oven to 450°F with two sheet pans on the top and bottom racks.

2. Bring a large pot of salted water to a boil for pasta. For the sauce, in a large skillet over medium heat, add 1 tablespoon of the olive oil. When the oil is hot, add the garlic and let sizzle until just golden on the edges, about 1 minute. Season with red pepper flakes. Add the tomatoes and 2 cups water. Bring to a simmer and cook until slightly thickened (this should be a little looser than most tomato sauces), about 10 minutes. Stir in the basil, season with salt, and keep warm.

3. In a large bowl, toss the mushrooms, zucchini, and bell pepper with the remaining 2 tablespoons olive oil and season with salt. Spread on the two preheated sheet pans and roast, stirring and rotating the sheets from top to bottom once, until the vegetables are browned and tender, 20 to 25 minutes. Let the vegetables cool until just warm. Scrape the cooled vegetables into a large bowl and mix in the ricotta, cottage cheese, and ¼ cup of the Grana Padano. In a small bowl, toss together the mozzarella and the remaining ½ cup Grana Padano.

4. Meanwhile, add the shells to the boiling water. When the pasta is very al dente, drain, rinse, then pat dry.

5. Spread about 1½ cups sauce in the bottom of a 13-by-9-inch glass or ceramic baking dish. Fill the shells with the vegetable mixture and arrange in the baking dish. Ladle the remaining sauce over the shells and top with the grated cheese mixture. Cover with aluminum foil (not touching the actual shells) and bake until the sauce is bubbly, about 15 minutes. Uncover and bake until the cheese is browned and bubbly, about 15 minutes more.

Baked Elbows with Butternut Squash Sauce

Think of this as an Italian twist on mac and cheese, with the pureed squash substituting for the extra cheese, milk, and butter usually found in dishes like this. Be careful when blending hot liquids like this sauce—remove the plastic center piece of the blender top to allow steam to escape and cover the top of the blender with a kitchen towel.

CALORIES PER SERVING:
490

1 small butternut squash, peeled and cubed (3 cups)

1½ cups low-sodium chicken broth

1½ cups 1% low-fat milk

3 garlic cloves, crushed and peeled

1 fresh rosemary sprig

1 fresh bay leaf

2 tablespoons heavy cream

Kosher salt and freshly ground black pepper

1 pound elbow macaroni

7 ounces freshly grated Italian fontina

¼ cup panko bread crumbs

¼ cup freshly grated Grana Padano

¼ cup fresh Italian parsley leaves, chopped

2 teaspoons extra-virgin olive oil

1. Preheat the oven to 400°F.

2. Bring a large pot of salted water to a boil for pasta. In a medium saucepan, combine the squash, chicken broth, milk, garlic, rosemary, and bay leaf. Bring to a simmer over medium heat and cook until the squash is very tender, 10 to 12 minutes. Cool slightly, remove the bay leaf and rosemary, and pour into a blender. Pour in the cream and blend carefully until smooth. Season with salt and pepper.

3. Meanwhile, add the elbows to the boiling water. When the pasta is al dente, drain, reserving 1 cup pasta water in a cup. Return the pasta to the pasta pot, add the sauce, toss the pasta and sauce with the grated fontina, and season with salt and pepper. Add a little pasta water, if necessary, to coat all of the pasta in the sauce.

4. Pour into a 13-by-9-inch glass or ceramic baking dish. In a small bowl, toss together the panko, Grana Padano, parsley, and olive oil. Season with salt and pepper. Sprinkle over the pasta. Bake until the sauce is bubbly on the edges and the top is browned and crispy, 15 to 20 minutes (don't overbake or it will dry out).

SERVES 6

Mixed Bean Soup with Farfalline

We use cannellini and kidney beans as the base of this soup because they have about the same cooking times, but you could substitute other beans as long as their cooking times are similar—chickpeas take longer than all other beans, so don't use those. If you are making this soup ahead of time, prepare it up to the point where you add the farfalline. Reheat gently and cook the pasta in the soup right before serving. (If using gluten-free pasta here, cook it separately, until very al dente, and stir it in gently before serving.)

CALORIES PER SERVING:
395

½ cup dried cannellini beans

½ cup dried kidney beans

¼ cup extra-virgin olive oil

1 medium onion, chopped

2 medium carrots, chopped

2 celery stalks, chopped

1 tablespoon fresh thyme leaves, chopped

4 garlic cloves, chopped

3 tablespoons tomato paste

1 (3-inch) piece Grana Padano rind

2 fresh bay leaves

1 small head escarole, chopped

½ cup brown lentils, rinsed

Kosher salt and freshly ground black pepper

1 cup farfalline

1 cup fresh Italian parsley leaves, chopped

6 tablespoons freshly grated Grana Padano

1. Soak the cannellini and kidney beans in cold water overnight. Drain and rinse.

2. In a medium Dutch oven over medium heat, add 3 tablespoons of olive oil. When the oil is hot, add the onion, carrots, and celery and cook until the onion is almost tender, about 8 minutes. Add the thyme and garlic and cook until fragrant, about 1 minute. Make a space in the pan and add the tomato paste. Let toast a minute or two, then stir the tomato paste into the vegetables. Add 3 quarts water, the cheese rind, and bay leaves and bring to a simmer.

3. When the soup is simmering, add the soaked beans. Cook, covered, until the beans are almost tender, 50 minutes to 1 hour.

4. Uncover, add the escarole and lentils, and simmer until all of the beans are tender, 25 to 35 minutes. Season with salt and pepper. If the soup seems very thick, add 1 to 2 cups of water. Add the farfalline and parsley and cook until very al dente (the pasta will cook more in the pot off the heat). Remove the bay leaves. Stir in the remaining 1 tablespoon olive oil. Serve in soup bowls, sprinkling each serving with 1 tablespoon grated Grana Padano.

SERVES 6

Tomato Clam Chowder with Pastina

Steaming the clams (as opposed to using chopped canned clams) gives you a flavorful base to use for your soup, so don't skip this step. The chowder could be made ahead, but add the cooked clams and pastina when you reheat to serve.

CALORIES PER SERVING:
326

3 tablespoons extra-virgin olive oil

6 garlic cloves, crushed and peeled

2 fresh bay leaves

4 fresh thyme sprigs

4 fresh Italian parsley sprigs, plus ½ cup leaves, chopped

½ cup dry white wine

2½ dozen littleneck clams

2 ounces pancetta, diced

1 medium onion, chopped (about 1 cup)

1 large carrot, chopped (about 1 cup)

2 celery stalks, chopped (about 1 cup)

Kosher salt

Crushed red pepper flakes

1 (28-ounce) can whole San Marzano tomatoes, crushed by hand

1 large russet potato, peeled and diced (about 3 cups)

¾ cup pastina

½ cup fresh basil leaves

1. In a Dutch oven over medium-high heat, add 1 tablespoon of the olive oil. When the oil is hot, add the garlic, a bay leaf, the thyme sprigs, and parsley sprigs. Once the herbs are sizzling, add the white wine and bring to a simmer. Add the clams, cover, and steam just until all of the clams open (if some open before others, remove to a bowl so that they don't overcook), about 8 minutes. Discard any clams that don't open. Remove all of the clams to a bowl and let cool enough to remove the meat. Chop the meat and reserve. (You should have about 1 heaping cup.) Strain the cooking juices. (You should have about 1 cup; if you have less, add water to make 1 cup. If you have more, reduce the water in step 3 by that extra amount.)

2. Wipe out the pot and add the remaining 2 tablespoons olive oil over medium heat. Add the pancetta and cook until the fat is rendered, about 4 minutes. Add the onion, carrot, and celery and cook until the onion is softened, about 8 minutes. Season with salt and red pepper flakes.

3. Add the tomatoes, the clam cooking juices, the remaining bay leaf, and 7 cups hot water. Bring to a simmer and cook for 10 minutes to blend the flavors. Add the potato and cook until just tender, about 10 minutes. Add the pastina, the remaining chopped parsley, and the basil, torn into pieces. When the pastina is still quite al dente, add the chopped clams. Simmer until the clams are just heated through, about 2 minutes, remove the bay leaves, and serve.

SERVES 6

Zucchini and Leek Soup with Pastina

This soup can be made ahead, but don't add the pastina until you're ready to serve or it will soak up all of the broth. The parsley garnish at the end adds a big boost of flavor and freshness.

CALORIES PER SERVING:
278

¼ cup extra-virgin olive oil

2 medium leeks, white and light green parts, thinly sliced (about 1 cup)

1 large carrot, diced

2 celery stalks, diced

Kosher salt and freshly ground black pepper

3 medium zucchini, diced (about 4 cups)

2 medium russet potatoes, peeled and cut into ½-inch dice (about 4 cups)

2 teaspoons fresh thyme leaves, chopped

2 quarts low-sodium chicken broth

2 fresh bay leaves

1 (3-inch) piece Grana Padano rind

1 cup pastina

1 cup fresh Italian parsley leaves

2 garlic cloves, crushed and peeled

6 tablespoons freshly grated Grana Padano

1. In a medium Dutch oven over medium heat, add 3 tablespoons of the olive oil. When the oil is hot, add the leeks, carrot, and celery and cook, without browning, until softened, about 10 minutes. Season with salt and pepper.

2. Add the zucchini and cook, without browning, until softened, about 6 minutes. Add the potatoes and cook just until they begin to stick to the bottom of the pot, about 4 minutes. Add the thyme and cook until fragrant, about 1 minute.

3. Pour in the chicken broth and 2 cups water and add the bay leaves and cheese rind. Bring the soup to a simmer and cook until the potatoes begin to fall apart and the soup has thickened, about 18 minutes. Add the pastina and cook until very al dente (it will continue to cook after the heat is off).

4. For the garnish, finely chop the parsley and garlic together with a pinch of salt and put in a small bowl. Stir in the remaining 1 tablespoon olive oil. To serve the soup, remove the cheese rind and bay leaves, stir in the parsley-garlic paste, and simmer for 1 minute. Sprinkle each serving with 1 tablespoon of the grated Grana Padano.

SERVES 6

Lemon Orzo Salad with Carrots, Bell Pepper, Celery, and Herbs

Dicing the vegetables to match the size of the orzo is not only pleasing to the eye, it distributes their flavor more evenly throughout the salad. This salad will benefit from being made at least a couple of hours ahead, but add the cheese and almonds right before serving so that they don't get soggy. Save a few tablespoons of the dressing to toss in at the last minute to freshen up the salad.

CALORIES PER SERVING:
422

1 pound orzo

Zest and juice of 2 lemons
(about ¼ cup juice)

1 teaspoon Dijon mustard

Kosher salt and freshly ground
black pepper

¼ cup extra-virgin olive oil

1 medium red bell pepper,
finely diced (about 1 cup)

2 large carrots, coarsely grated
(about 2 cups)

2 celery stalks, finely diced,
plus some celery leaves (about
1 cup)

1 bunch scallions, finely
chopped (about 1 cup)

1 cup mixed fresh soft herbs (a
combination of any, some, or
all—basil, parsley, chives, dill,
mint, and chervil), chopped

½ cup sliced or slivered
blanched almonds, toasted

1 (3-ounce) piece ricotta salata

I. Bring a large pot of salted water to a boil for pasta. Add the orzo to the boiling water. When the pasta is al dente, drain and cool under cold running water. Pat very dry on kitchen towels and put in a large serving bowl.

2. In a small bowl, whisk together the lemon juice and mustard and season with salt and pepper. Whisk in the olive oil in a slow, steady stream to make a smooth, emulsified dressing. Stir in the lemon zest.

3. To the orzo, add the bell pepper, carrots, celery (including leaves), scallions, and herbs. Drizzle with all but 2 tablespoons of the dressing. Season with salt and pepper. Cover with plastic wrap and refrigerate for several hours to let the flavors blend. Remove from the refrigerator about 30 minutes before you are ready to serve. Add the almonds and the reserved dressing and toss well. Shave the ricotta salata over the salad with a vegetable peeler, and toss gently, taking care not to break up the cheese too much. Serve immediately.

SERVES 6

Summer Couscous Salad with Crunchy Vegetables

To make this dish heartier, add about 3 ounces of cooked shrimp or grilled boneless, skinless chicken breast per person. It adds only 80 to 100 calories per serving and makes this a full meal. Couscous is actually a type of pasta—made with just semolina flour and water.

CALORIES PER SERVING:
465

3 cups low-sodium chicken broth

7 tablespoons extra-virgin olive oil

1½ cups whole wheat couscous

1 medium red bell pepper, diced (about 1 cup)

1 medium carrot, diced (about 1 cup)

2 celery stalks, diced (about 1 cup)

1 cup chopped scallions

1 small fennel bulb, cored and finely chopped (about 1½ cups), fronds reserved

1 cup large pitted green olives (such as Cerignola), slivered

Zest and juice of 2 lemons (about ¼ cup juice)

Kosher salt and freshly ground black pepper

½ cup fresh Italian parsley leaves, chopped

½ cup fresh basil leaves, chopped

1. In a medium saucepan, bring the chicken broth and 1 tablespoon of the olive oil to a simmer. Add the couscous, cover, and remove from the heat. Let sit, covered, for 5 minutes, then fluff well with a fork. Scrape onto a sheet pan to cool.

2. In a serving bowl, combine the cooled couscous, bell pepper, carrot, celery, scallions, chopped fennel, and olives. Drizzle with the lemon juice and the remaining 6 tablespoons olive oil and add the lemon zest. Toss well to coat all of the couscous with the dressing. Season with salt and pepper and add the parsley and basil. Chop ½ cup reserved fennel fronds and add that as well. Toss one more time and serve. The salad can also be made ahead and refrigerated, but let come to room temperature and toss again before serving.

SERVES 6

Pasta Salad with String Beans and Cherry Tomatoes

We use some of the grape tomatoes in this salad to make the dressing, cutting oil and calories and adding flavor and body to the vinaigrette. This is one time when it's okay to rinse pasta after cooking. You need to cool the pasta quickly and get rid of excess starch before tossing the pasta with the dressing. This salad can be chilled after assembling, but is best served at room temperature.

CALORIES PER SERVING:
476

3 cups grape tomatoes, halved

¾ cup fresh basil leaves

¼ cup red wine vinegar

1 small garlic clove, crushed and peeled

Pinch of sugar

Kosher salt and freshly ground black pepper

¼ cup extra-virgin olive oil

1 pound rotini or fusilli

12 ounces string beans, trimmed and cut into 1-inch lengths

8 ounces fresh mozzarella pearls

1. Bring a large pot of salted water to a boil for pasta. For the dressing, in a blender, combine ½ cup of the tomatoes, ¼ cup of the basil, the vinegar, and garlic. Season with the sugar, salt, and pepper. Blend until smooth. Add 1 tablespoon water and blend again. With the blender running, pour the olive oil through the top in a slow, steady stream to make a smooth, emulsified dressing. Pour the dressing into a large serving bowl.

2. Add the rotini to the boiling water. When the pasta is just beginning to soften, add the green beans and cook until both are al dente, 4 to 5 minutes. Drain and cool both under cold running water. Pat dry on kitchen towels.

3. Add the pasta and green beans to the serving bowl with the remaining 2½ cups tomatoes and the mozzarella and toss well. Chop the remaining ½ cup basil, add to the salad, and toss again. Serve immediately, or cover and chill until ready to serve. Remove from the refrigerator 30 minutes before you want to serve the pasta salad.

SERVES 6

Pasta Salad with Tuna and Boiled Eggs

Giardiniera is a variety of pickled Italian vegetables (usually cauliflower, pearl onions, celery, carrots, and bell peppers) available at most grocery stores and delis. It comes pickled in brine and is very low in calories. It's ready to use right out of the jar to add a quick jolt of flavor to salads, pasta, and sandwiches or as part of an antipasti spread.

CALORIES PER SERVING:
498

4 large eggs

1 pound penne

2 (15-ounce) jars giardiniera, drained and chopped (about 3 cups), plus 6 tablespoons brine from the jar

2 tablespoons red wine vinegar

3 tablespoons low-fat mayonnaise

¼ cup extra-virgin olive oil

Kosher salt and freshly ground black pepper

2 (5-ounce) cans white tuna in spring water, drained

½ cup pitted green Italian olives (such as Cerignola), slivered (about 15)

½ cup roasted red peppers in brine, drained and chopped

1 cup fresh Italian parsley leaves, chopped

1. In a small saucepan, add the eggs with water to cover by about 1 inch. Bring the water to a boil, then immediately reduce the heat so that the water is barely simmering. Simmer for 10 minutes, then drain and add the eggs to a bowl of ice water to cool completely. Peel and cut into rough chunks.

2. Bring a large pot of water to a boil for pasta. Add the penne to the boiling water. When the pasta is al dente, drain, reserve ½ cup pasta water, rinse under cold running water until the pasta is cool, then pat very dry on kitchen towels.

3. In a large serving bowl, whisk together 2 tablespoons of the giardiniera brine, the vinegar, mayonnaise, and olive oil. Season with salt and pepper. Add the chopped giardiniera and crumble in the tuna. Add the olives, red peppers, and pasta. Toss well to coat everything with the dressing. Add the parsley and eggs and toss gently. Add up to ¼ cup more giardiniera brine if the salad seems dry. The salad is best if it is allowed to sit at room temperature for 30 minutes before serving to let the flavors develop. If the salad seems dry after it has been sitting, drizzle in enough reserved pasta water to moisten and toss once more before serving.

SERVES 6

Farfalle with Creamy Tuna Sauce, Lemon, and Capers

This is a lower-calorie version of the classic Italian tonnato sauce, which is usually used as a dressing for cold veal. Here, it dresses pasta and crunchy raw vegetables. This is best served at room temperature as more of a pasta salad.

CALORIES PER SERVING:
384

1 pound farfalle

1 (5-ounce) can white tuna in spring water, drained

Juice of 1 lemon

2 tablespoons capers in brine, drained

2 anchovy fillets

1 small garlic clove

3 tablespoons low-fat mayonnaise

3 tablespoons extra-virgin olive oil

Kosher salt and freshly ground black pepper

3 celery stalks, thinly sliced (about 1½ cups)

2 medium carrots, chopped (about 1½ cups)

1 small fennel bulb, sliced (about 1½ cups), plus 1 cup fronds, chopped

1 cup fresh Italian parsley leaves, coarsely chopped

1. Bring a large pot of salted water to a boil for pasta. Add the farfalle to the boiling water. When the pasta is al dente, drain, rinse, and pat dry on kitchen towels. Transfer to a serving bowl.

2. In the work bowl of a food processor, combine the tuna, lemon juice, capers, anchovies, garlic, and mayonnaise. Process to make a smooth paste, scraping down the sides of the work bowl. With the machine running, pour in the olive oil and process to make a smooth dressing. Add enough cold water (about 2 tablespoons) to make the dressing pourable, about the consistency of pancake batter. Season with salt and pepper. Pour over the farfalle and toss well. Add the celery, carrots, sliced fennel, chopped fronds, and parsley and toss well to combine. Serve at room temperature.

SERVES 6

Niçoise Pasta Salad

The addition of the chicken broth helps to make enough dressing to coat the pasta, without using too much olive oil. Classic Niçoise salad has boiled new potatoes, but you don't need that extra starch because there's pasta here.

CALORIES PER SERVING:
452

1 pound cavatappi

8 ounces haricots verts, trimmed and halved crosswise

3 tablespoons red wine vinegar

1 tablespoon Dijon mustard

3 anchovy fillets

1 garlic clove, crushed and peeled

¼ cup low-sodium chicken broth

6 tablespoons extra-virgin olive oil

3 medium ripe plum tomatoes, seeded and chopped (about 1½ cups)

1 cup fresh Italian parsley leaves, chopped

2 (5-ounce) cans solid white tuna in water, drained and flaked

Kosher salt and freshly ground black pepper

3 hard-boiled eggs, peeled and coarsely chopped

¼ cup pitted, halved Niçoise olives (about 16)

I. Bring a large pot of salted water to a boil for pasta. Add the cavatappi to the boiling water. After 7 minutes, add the haricots verts. When the pasta is al dente and the haricots verts are crisp-tender, drain, reserving ½ cup pasta water, and cool the pasta and haricots verts under running water. Pat dry on kitchen towels and put in a large serving bowl.

2. In the work bowl of a mini food processor, combine the vinegar, mustard, anchovies, garlic, and chicken broth and puree until smooth. With the machine running, pour in the olive oil in a steady stream to make an emulsified dressing.

3. Pour half of the dressing over the pasta and toss. Add the tomatoes, parsley, and tuna, and drizzle with the remaining dressing. Season with salt and pepper and toss well. Scatter the eggs and olives on top and serve.

SERVES 6

Breakfast Pasta Frittata

Serve this frittata for breakfast or brunch, with a side of roasted potatoes and some fresh fruit.

CALORIES PER SERVING:
383

3 tablespoons extra-virgin olive oil

8 ounces turkey breakfast sausage links, removed from casings

1 medium red bell pepper, sliced

2 cups chopped scallions

Kosher salt and freshly ground black pepper

5 large eggs

5 large egg whites

⅓ cup nonfat milk

1 cup fresh Italian parsley leaves, chopped

½ cup freshly grated mild Cheddar cheese

¼ cup freshly grated Grana Padano

8 ounces spaghetti (or other long pasta), cooked and cooled

1. Preheat the broiler.

2. In a medium nonstick ovenproof skillet over medium heat, add 1 tablespoon of the olive oil. When the oil is hot, add the sausage and cook and crumble with a fork until cooked through, about 4 minutes. Remove to a small bowl. Add the bell pepper to the skillet and cook until almost tender, about 6 minutes. Add the scallions and cook until wilted, about 3 minutes. Scrape the sausage back into the pan and season with salt and pepper.

3. In a large bowl, whisk together the eggs, egg whites, and milk until smooth. Season with salt and pepper. Whisk in the parsley, Cheddar, and Grana Padano, reserving 1 tablespoon of each cheese for the top of the frittata.

4. Heat the skillet over medium-high heat and add the remaining 2 tablespoons olive oil. Add the spaghetti to the sausage and vegetables and stir to coat with the oil. Cook, stirring occasionally, until the spaghetti is golden in places, about 3 minutes. Pour in the egg mixture and let cook until the bottom is set, about 6 minutes.

5. Sprinkle the top with the remaining 2 tablespoons grated cheese. Broil until the top is golden but not dry or wrinkly and the frittata is cooked through, 3 to 4 minutes, but watch carefully—all broilers are different. Let cool in the pan for 10 minutes, then slide onto a cutting board and cut into wedges. Serve warm or at room temperature.

SERVES 6

Spaghetti and Onion Frittata

This a very basic frittata, lightened by substituting egg whites for half of the eggs. We like to make this dish to use up leftover pasta that has already been sauced. Just add as directed in the recipe, but check before adding salt as the pasta will already have some seasoning. This recipe has room for a few extra calories, so you can vary the frittata by adding leftover roasted vegetables or a little cooked lean meat, such as crumbled turkey sausage. A little goes a long way in a frittata, so don't add more than one cup of "extras."

If you are watching your fat intake, use part-skim ricotta from the grocery store, but be sure to drain it. The draining concentrates flavor and takes out the excess liquid, which could otherwise make the frittata soggy. You can skip this step if you use fresh ricotta from an Italian deli; it's already thick enough, though it will be higher in calories and fat.

CALORIES PER SERVING:
389

¾ cup part-skim ricotta

¼ cup extra-virgin olive oil

2 medium onions, thinly sliced (about 2 cups)

Pinch of sugar

Kosher salt and freshly ground black pepper

5 large eggs

5 large egg whites

⅓ cup nonfat milk

1 cup fresh Italian parsley leaves, chopped

½ cup freshly grated Grana Padano

8 ounces spaghetti (or other long pasta), cooked and cooled

1. Put the ricotta in a small strainer lined with cheesecloth (or simply a very fine strainer without cheesecloth). Set over a bowl and let drain in the refrigerator for a couple of hours. Discard the liquid in the bottom of the bowl.

2. Preheat the broiler.

3. In a medium nonstick ovenproof skillet over medium heat, add 2 tablespoons of the olive oil. When the oil is hot, add the onions and pinch of sugar. Stir to coat the onions in the oil and season with salt and pepper. Cook, stirring occasionally, over medium heat until the onions are wilted and dark golden, about 25 minutes. Scrape onto a plate. Wipe the skillet clean with a paper towel.

4. In a large bowl, whisk together the eggs, egg whites, and milk until smooth. Season with salt and pepper. Whisk in the parsley and grated Grana Padano, reserving 1 tablespoon cheese for the top of the frittata.

5. Heat the skillet over medium-high heat and add the remaining 2 tablespoons olive oil. Add the spaghetti and stir to coat with the oil. Cook, stirring occasionally, until the spaghetti is golden in places, about 3 min-

utes. Add the onions and stir to incorporate. Pour in the egg mixture and let cook until the bottom is set, about 6 minutes.

6. Dollop the ricotta in spoonfuls evenly over the top of the frittata. Sprinkle with the remaining 1 tablespoon grated Grana Padano. Broil until the top is golden but not dry or wrinkly and the frittata is cooked through, 3 to 4 minutes, but watch carefully—all broilers are different. Let cool in the pan for 10 minutes, then slide onto a cutting board and cut into wedges. Serve warm or at room temperature.

SERVES 6

Acknowledgments

There are so many people to thank after such a wonderful collaboration on a book. A big thank-you and much gratitude to Peter Gethers and Christina Malach for your stimulating ideas and guidance; without your input, this book would never have come into being. Thank you to Jenna Brickley for not letting any of the details escape us. Deep appreciation for the cooking, measuring, and great attention to detail goes to Amy Stevenson, who really makes a book like this happen; after many years of friendship, it is always an honor to be able to work with you.

For making it all look so delicious and beautiful, a deep-hearted thank-you to Steve Giralt; your photographs are exquisite. Missy Davis, your organization and wonderful personality made the long days of photography a pleasure and a real breeze—thank you. And a special thanks to Penelope Bouklas for bringing very pretty and really perfect things in which to serve and photograph the food. It all looks so wonderful. Last, but certainly and most definitely not least, thank you, Cody Hogan, for your undying dedication to good food and to our family. You are a true treasure and a pleasure to work with. The food looked gorgeous and, as the group doing photography knows, tasted wonderful as well.

Thank you to the team at Knopf that pulls it all together and makes it all look so beautiful. It is always a pleasure to work with Kristen Bearse, and beyond her being a pleasure, her keen eye and sense of design are incomparable. Kelly Blair, thank you for making the jacket look wonderful and knowing what we want in order to put our best foot forward. Thank you also to Kathleen Fridella, our production editor, and Lisa Montebello, our production manager. For getting it out there, a thank-you goes to Erinn McGrath and, of course, Paul Bogaards for always being such a big supporter of all that we do.

A special thank-you to our mother, Lidia, who instilled in us a strong work ethic, love of family, and passion for food. However, the most heartfelt thanks go to our five children collectively (Lorenzo, Julia, Olivia, Miles, and Ethan) for being the wonderful people you are and for eating all that pasta!

Index

Page references in *italics* refer to illustrations.

A Note About Joe

Joe Bastianich is one of America's preeminent restaurateurs and TV personalities; he is also an author, musician, and triathlete. He and his mother, Lidia Bastianich, and Mario Batali are the owners of twenty-five restaurants globally and partners in Eataly, the world's largest Italian artisanal marketplace. In 2005 Joe was recognized as an Outstanding Wine and Spirits Professional by both the James Beard Foundation and *Bon Appétit,* and in 2008 he and Mario were awarded the James Beard Foundation's Outstanding Restaurateur Award. He has coauthored two award-winning books on Italian wine, and his highly anticipated memoir, *Restaurant Man,* became a *New York Times* best seller in its first week of release in May 2012. Joe was a judge on U.S. *MasterChef,* along with Gordon Ramsay and chef Graham Elliot, and in 2011 he joined as a judge on *MasterChef Italia.* His most recent TV role is on the CNBC reality show *Restaurant Startup,* a food-and-restaurant-business-themed series giving budding entrepreneurs the chance to make their dreams come true by securing an investment from Joe and his partner chef Tim Love. When Joe is not whipping up new business deals or working the dining room at one of his many restaurants, he can be found at his home in Greenwich, Connecticut, playing guitar and spending time with his wife, Deanna, and their three children.

A Note About Tanya

Tanya Bastianich Manuali's visits to Italy as a child sparked her passion for the country's art and culture. She dedicated herself to the study of Italian Renaissance art during her college years at Georgetown, and earned a master's degree from Syracuse University and a doctorate from Oxford University. Living and studying in many regions of Italy, she taught art history to American students in Florence, although she met her husband, Corrado Manuali, who is from Rome, in New York City. Tanya co-owns and is an executive producer of Tavola Productions, producing Lidia's public television show, among others, and is active daily in the family restaurant businesses. She leads the development of the Lidia brand social media and merchandising. Together with her husband, Corrado, Tanya oversees the production and expansion of Lidia's food line, which includes ten cuts of pasta and seven sauces. Tanya has coauthored five books with her mother: *Lidia's Commonsense Italian Cooking, Lidia's Favorite Recipes, Lidia's Italy, Lidia Cooks from the Heart of Italy,* and *Lidia's Italy in America.* In 2010, Tanya coauthored *Reflections of the Breast: Breast Cancer in Art Through the Ages,* a social–art historical look at breast cancer in art from ancient Egypt to today. Tanya and Corrado live in New York City with their children, Lorenzo and Julia.

A Note on the Type

The text of this book was set in Chaparral, a typeface designed in 2000 by Carol Twombly, one of the most influential designers of the late twentieth century. The original inspiration for Chaparral was a page of lettering found in a sixteenth-century manuscript. As she was digitizing the lettering for the Adobe corporation, Twombly saw that it could be adapted into a readable slab serif design. Chaparral captures the essence of the sixteenth-century style while introducing a warmer, contemporary feel.

Composed by North Market Street Graphics,
Lancaster, Pennsylvania

Printed and bound by RR Donnelley,
Crawfordsville, Indiana

Designed by M. Kristen Bearse